AF580023

The Weight of the Image

4th International NAI Summer Master class
15 – 28 August 1999
Netherlands Architecture Institute, Rotterdam

Lars Spuybroek (NOX)
Bob Lang (ARUP)

Bob Lang
Lars Spuybroek

Foreword

One of my first concerns since taking up the position of director of the NAI in spring 1996 was to provide young architects greater access to the institute and its exciting potential as a thought-provoking place for dialogue and innovation. What I wanted to establish was a framework for an open and creative exchange between architects, both students and young professionals, and internationally experienced teachers. The idea of an annual summer workshop, two weeks of concentrated discussion and production, seemed an ideal way to start.

Since 1996 until now there have been a series of master classes with inspiring and provoking architects and tutors, like Thom Mayne/Morphosis (Los Angeles), Wiel Arets (Maastricht), Mattias Sauerbruch (Berlin), Kees Christiaanse (Rotterdam), Lebbeus Woods (New York) and Jos Bosman (Zürich). They all started intensive dialogues with students from all over the world.

The NAI Summer Master class 1999 **The Weight of the Image** was supervised by Lars Spuybroek of NOX (Rotterdam) and the engineer Bob Lang from ARUP (London). They formed a congenial team and worked together with 30 architecture students and young architects from eleven countries. Fifteen teams of two students designed and detailed stadiums using animation software and three-dimensional models.

The spirit of the workshop throughout, and the results were highly remarkable and I am sure that this booklet reflects that clearly, just as it showcases new possibilities in architectural design using computer programming. I am therefore very pleased that we have been able to compile the process of the NAI Summer Master class 1999 into this publication.

Lastly my sincere thanks to Lars Spuybroek and Bob Lang for their engagement in this project.

Kristin Feireiss
Director, Netherlands Architecture Institute

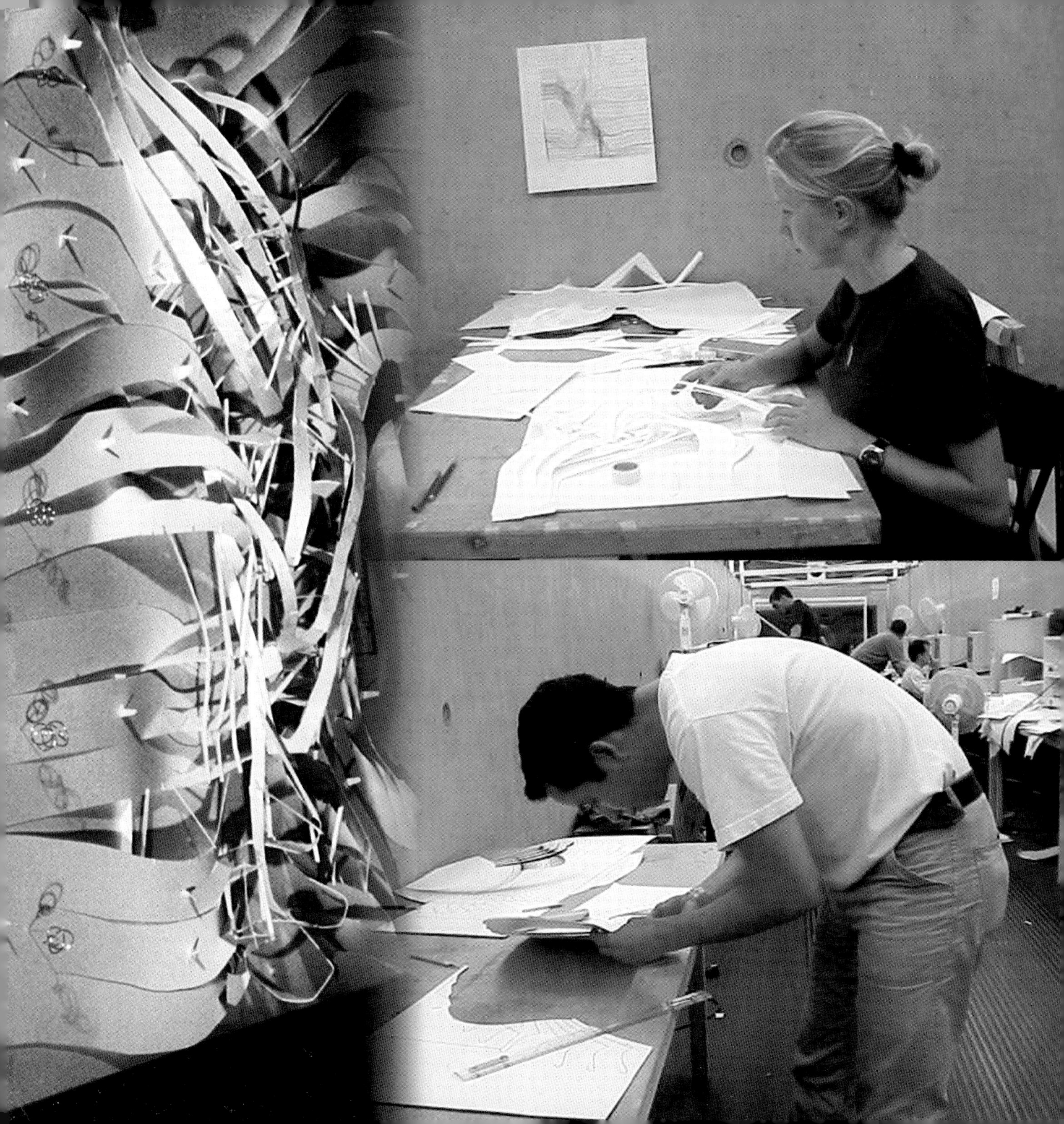

MACHINING ARCHITECTURE

Lars Spuybroek

Workshops are an enormous luxury – to teachers, that is. Especially in the form of master classes. The limited amount of time makes it suddenly possible to get students to do almost anything, things otherwise unimaginable... Because every act is haunted, if not propelled, by the lack of time, all the obligatory hesitations and deliberations are virtually absent, and the teacher finds himself freed from all Socratic maneuvering, the perpetual negotiating and persuading that is so characteristic of teaching design students.

We immediately took this inherent courage as a basis to focus on methodology and design technique, instead of experimenting with form, as is customary. Workshops are usually opposed to techniques, meant instead to personalize the design process which is then later – in a classroom situation – filtered through the more collective means of objective techniques. Generally one is taught "freedom" at the beginning of the process, the level of conceptualization, and "discipline" at the later stages of design, the level of materialization. Here, we decided to employ a regime of procedural steps to teach precision, especially at the start of the design process. I think it is most urgent to teach discipline at the conceptual level, not to clear out any of the necessary vagueness that goes with every beginning but to develop tools to instrumentalize that un-knowing and make it productive in a field of knowledge.

diagramming – the porosity of the image

In the last ten or fifteen years, there has been an important shift away from teaching all kinds of preliminary techniques like sketching and modeling toward diagramming – developing non-visual drawing techniques that are based not on optical abstractions of later-to-be-realized forms but on informational visualization techniques that place themselves at the interior of a process instead of the exterior of a sensed form. The diagram is a very clearly lined network of relationships, but it is completely vague in its formal expression. Diagrams love pulp, and they only recognize materials at their most heated and their weakest stages. The diagram is basically a conceptual input/output device which swallows matter and, while restructuring, also ejects matter. In that sense, every informational plane is always an interface between material states. That's why it functions totally differently from the classic reduction-production pair, where the sketch is always frustrated and slowed down by materialization, by development, either in the later stages of the design process, or later when built and experienced. Somehow, the sketch was always better. The diagram, on the other hand, is an engine, a motor: it doesn't want to impose itself on matter, but to engage in a process of continuous formation – it operates at the backside of the image, on its blind side. Diagrams are the informational nodes and codes of the world; they are stabilizing contractions in material flows – first they channel and then they relax. They are faces in a landscape, singular perceptions connecting streams of actions. They are lenses, mirroring a movement: first a contraction of matter-energy onto an organizing surface, then an expansion into many new other structures.

- contraction – a movement of virtualization, where information is gathered, selected, graphed, and then organized into a virtual machine: from a 3-D network towards a 2-D surface. A movement toward quality, order and organization.
- expansion – a movement of actualization, where the organizational diagram is put inside matter, where it germinates and becomes formative: from a 2-D surface towards a 3-D structure. A movement toward quantity, matter and structure.

Obviously computing is nothing but an enhancement (on top of language) of the communication between diagrams, a meta-diagramming, to potentially connect all actions on matter. A prediagrammed world that doesn't make us leave our bodies, but does exactly the opposite – produces more and more material events with more and more variation, like an electronic rain forest, steadily replacing the realm of work with the realm of design. An easy guideline to how much information a form contains is the amount of text needed to describe it. But as every architect knows, a lot of what is "written" by designers is pre-stated, pre-articulated (program, building materials, coding, zoning, etc.). I think the electronic networking of the world is nothing but a tendency away from this advance molding, and more and more architectural programs will become vaguer, more and more building materials will lose their shape and become granulated. Everybody who teaches diagrams should teach theories of making (or reproduction), and this is why every school that teaches computer-aided design should also teach computer-aided conceptualization and computer-aided manufacturing.

In the material world, diagrams always hide themselves in processes (is there anything but a process?), but in the human world of design, they always take on the shape of surfaces, like memories or screens. As designers, we have always had to slip surfaces in. These have now evolved ***from visual surfaces towards operational surfaces***. In a sense, the image no longer shows the exterior of a system but must show the interior and exterior simultaneously, like an X-ray, but an abstracted X-ray in which all potential actions are contained in functions and parameters. As many others have observed, the larger cultural shift is one of surfaces towards interfaces: open, porous surfaces that are no longer images but nonetheless make use of visualization. These images aren't "seen," as in a passive recording technique, but precisely in an active way, where the seeing is permeated with acting. In this sense the diagram is a virtualization of action, a ***motor diagram*** which isn't a "plan" for what to do, but more a strategy, a fabric of action, where actions aren't prescribed, but only rules for interactions. In its first years, diagrams were still rather "visual" in the sense that they were often drawn from art or existing scientific imagery (of dynamic processes). But with the question of how to "translate them into form," they had to become more procedural, first by experimenting with different notational techniques, and now through computing, where we can finally connect thoughts directly to buttons. Buttons connected to other buttons, all connected to pencils, hundreds of them interactively drawing, simultaneously "thinking everything through."

Any dynamics can be analyzed by a diagram (afterwards, as with natural processes), but any diagram can be at the start of a process (beforehand, as with machines), so process and surface are interchangeable – one can be the result of the other. Machines can contain diagrams, and diagrams can contain each other. A screen can contain a machine that contains images, but the question is always this: How does a diagram expand in relation to what it has contracted? How is what is going into the machine related to what comes out of it? As this happens a priori over time, we should remember that the diagram exists first on the level of conception (how does it help to produce the form? How does it postpone the image? How can one postpone seeing?), and second on the level of perception and experience in the built form (how can the diagram be sensed in the building itself? How do behavior, habit and desire – our ***own*** motor diagrams – meet up with the design?). If that is the outcome, it should also contain exactly that: life and geometry. The geometry of life and the life of geometry. I think diagrams only work when both connect. All reading is wrong. There is no signification. We shouldn't separate building materials too much from our bodies; walls experience the architecture just as much as we do. We are a contracting diagram, ***a sense datum***, continuing the present in space. We are presentations of diagrams, not representations of types.

In the case of the master class, our procedural technique consisted of building an action-perception machine on the computer: that is, a combination of images (in architecture, generally positioned on the vertical) and movement (generally positioned on the horizontal) that, while it unfolds over time through interaction of its parts, produces geometrical structure as a diagram: all points in movement create lines, all lines in movement create surfaces, and everything in between. That means all movement, movements of and within movements, are written down as structures, and all events become structural events. All traces become paths, all paths make up landscapes. Paths have a tendency to form hierarchies; landscapes have a tendency to even them out. Together they make up a charged field of inclinations. The fixed interacts with the slippery, memory interacts with experience, not by rubbing their skins against each other, but internally, structurally. All things that develop in time show themselves simultaneously in space. All things in space unfold in time.

The idea was to design a "virtual stadium" as part of the existing Museumpark directly in front of the Netherlands Architecture Institute in Rotterdam. A year before Euro2000, the European football championships co-organized by the Netherlands and Belgium, it was foreseen that a large number of fans would be unable to attend the games and that it might be desirable to let them watch the matches virtually, on a enormous television screen, and collectively. To develop an aesthetics of crowd control. The setup was as follows: on the top floor of the Netherlands Architecture Institute we had two corridors at our disposal, each three meters wide, three meters high and 24 meters long. One was arranged for a "clean" first week, the other for a "dirtier" second week. The clean corridor contained fifteen high-powered PCs and 30 chairs. The other contained wooden tables, cardboard, paper and knives. 30 students (very talented and from all over the world) were paired off and handcuffed together, as in the early Hitchcocks, to learn digital design techniques in a five-step procedure. The first two steps involved contraction, the third the production of a flat surface, and the fourth and fifth were stages of expansion:

the first machine: drilling (inserting a screen in the designing mind/hand of a student) – a two day training in Maya (Alias/Wavefront). The first diagram is the computer; the second one is the type of software. Maya is the most integrative tool available today. Students can combine typical data analysis from programs like Excel (Microsoft Office) with image manipulations from stills or films from Adobe PhotoShop or Premiere and the amazing surface modeling tools in Maya. The drill emphasized time-based tools like Inverse Kinematics (skeletons with bones and joints, generally used to animate bodies such as running dinosaurs), Particle Dynamics (generally used to simulate snowstorms, fire and smoke, or flocks of birds) and Soft Body Dynamics (used for complex material behavior like fabric in the wind, rubber or jelly-like geometry interacting with other surfaces or force fields such as gravity, turbulence and vortex). One cannot overestimate the effect of this type of software on the minds of architecture students. They were especially trained in building interactive devices, where different effects affected each other and the whole – not like clockworks, but like bodies, where the parts influence the whole and the whole influences the parts.

the second machine: abstracting (inserting an interface at the start of a project) – building conceptual machines in Maya to organize information. We gave them a model, a machine that was "pre-contracted." Instead of having each team develop its own conceptual contraction into a machine, and run the risk of not being educated, we built a prototypical "cave." The cave was oversimplified (in a way we were sure would irritate the students) and also contained a lot of the givens of the project: a six-sided cube without no up or down orientation, with a camera projecting images on each side of the cube (as in the CAVE, or computer-aided virtual environment). These images consisted of typical park images (because of the site), typical crowd images (because of the match and the site) and typical media imagery (pan shots and close-ups combined with overviews within a stadium). Obviously this setup was not yet a machine; it could become one only when all static imagery was interpreted as the starting point for a new situation. Here, every student would experience the difference between the "old" diagramming technique of using images in the design process (and vaguely "translating" them) and the "new" one: putting the design process into a machine itself. Not taking one design decision after another, but taking 20 decisions and have the machine work it out simultaneously. For this, it is necessary to twist the relationship of geometry (static cube) and image (six series of six) into one of action (diagrammatic reading of the images) and geometry (an unfolding of the cube). While in our given cave the images and geometry weren't related, in the second – the machine designed by the students – they would have to be, because the images were interpreted as actions upon the geometry itself. Inevitably all images had to be "put into" the machine as parametric flows: the flows of the crowd on site, the course of the match, the movement of the cameras, the editing of the media event (close-ups, interviews, forecasts, replays, etc.). Because the images in the cave we supplied did not "see" each other, they did not respond to each other. They were just there, which is exactly why nothing happens in a Platonic cave: there is no relation between the cave and the images; the stone can't remember the image, and can't respond to new images coming in. The big question is then: What is the difference between the shape of the machine on frame zero (the start of the animation) and all the other frames (the rest of the animation as it unfolds in time)? In frame zero, the machine would still look a lot like the old type of diagram – a positioning of simple surfaces and objects related to each other by dotted lines, arrows and short instructive statements (if, then). The big difference, however, is that what is just a ***notation*** in the diagrammatic stage is an actual connection or ***action*** in the machine stage. An arrow is a real force, with size and direction; a dotted line is a real connection, either in the form of a "motion path" or a "spring" or "bone," and when instructions are executed they change position, direction and shape – and these changes result in a different processing of the instructions. The changes aren't added up but multiplied. All movement is processed as a whole, internally and externally. Each line isn't just translated and/or rotated (the basic mechanistic motions), but also transformed (shortened or lengthened) and bent. Students suddenly discover ***patterns between information and form***, patterns of repetitions and changes, in both time and space. All the later frames, especially when developing periodicity, give us an immediate geometrical

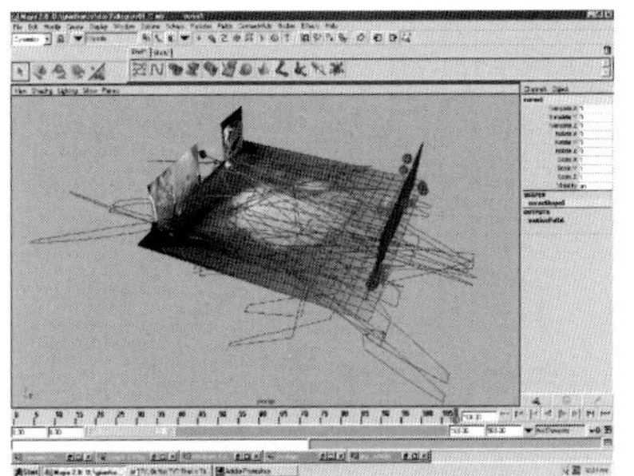
machine setup in Maya

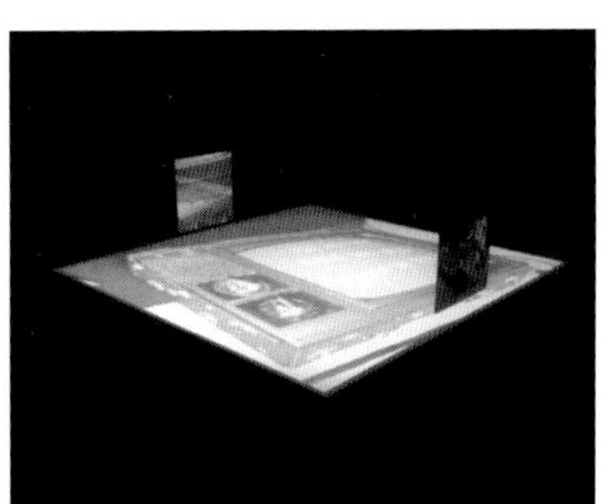
frame 0

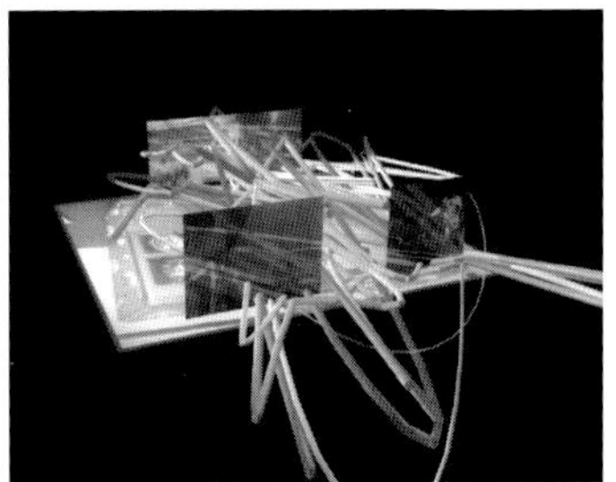
frame 138

expression of all "motor images" as they fluctuate over time: rotations, rotational deformations, stretchings, stretched twistings, splittings, twisted splittings, mergings within translations – all movement integrated, all images integrated in something that is not moving anymore... not visual anymore... Completely abstracted.

the third machine: surfacing (inserting a plane in architecture) – contracting the organizational model onto a surface. Look forward not back... Very important tutorial instruction: We don't judge the diagram at the level of its input, we judge it on its potential. If it is too formal, that is not good. If it's too visual, that's not good either.

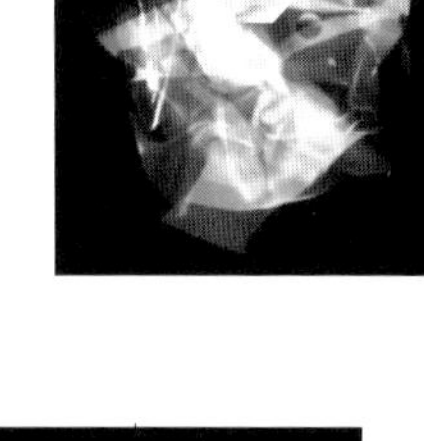

"Everyone make a print of your diagram tomorrow."

"What? But we're finally building machines like you asked us to, and now you want us to make flat prints!"

"Yes, and please do it with black lines on white paper, no fuss." (Secret empathy between the flat empty screen at the beginning, this paper surface at the end of the first week, and later in the second week, the ground level of the existing park.)

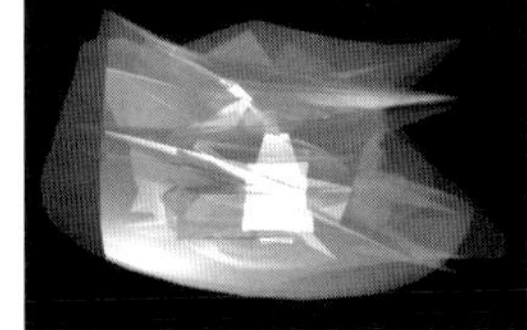

We all ooh and aah over the prints: beautiful, impossible X-rays, over-Pollocked, super-Forsythed, hyper-magnetic tracings, mappings of potentials. Lines flipping in and out of surfaces. Surfaces swallowed by lines. Surfaces acting like lines, like narrow bands, meeting up, splitting down. Finally, a look at architecture without a building blurring it! Just bring them onto the next level. No problem seeing trees, football, food, police, dogs, images, crowds, cars, fights – no problem at all.

the fourth machine: structuring (inserting a surface in the realm of volume) – literally giving the paper diagram volume by reworking it as a model. You should not just take the black lines seriously... the white paper is just as important. Instead of "translating" the diagram into what pre-exists in architecture (scale, site, materials, program), we apply the diagram first, before anything else, to the paper itself. Just a trick, nothing else. It prevents them from bluntly dragging everything in. Slowly materializing a diagram means realizing the diagram was never immaterial anyway; it is just a very heated, liquid sense of material, completely non-formal, extremely homogeneous, slowly to be cooled down and differentiated – first a step into paper/structure, then into cardboard/form... then concrete, steel, wood, whatever, in every mixture.

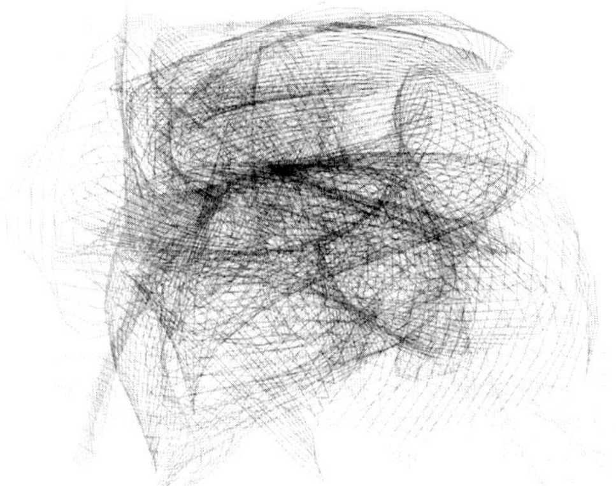

"We'll redraw the diagram with paper!" Bewildered faces. Every twist, every curve, every structural event on the paper should now happen to the paper itself. Paper bends, paper folds, paper cuts, paper

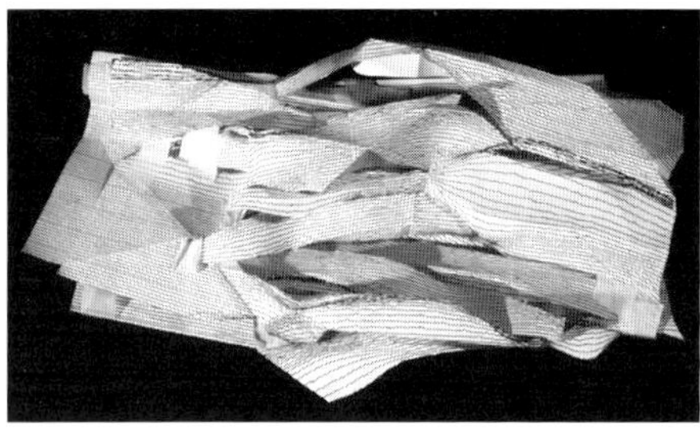

glues very easily too. They take the black lines as procedural instructions for the surface itself. This is not a move out of the computer, we should hasten to add. It is just material calculation, finding new rules, which later of course can be virtualized, even programmed. But this "move" is fundamentally one of becoming volume, but never as an elevation – we never jump a dimension; the act will be traced in a bridging of dimensions themselves. They are thickening the surface, a structural thickening, no need later for columns or walls. We get braids, bundles, cables, hair, hairdos, knots, proteins, weavings... Line volumes, line surfaces, surface volumes, hyperlines (lines out of lines), hypersurfaces (surfaces in surfaces). The diagram gets up and self-engineers.

the fifth machine: modeling (inserting a diagram on the level of built structures) – integrating structural properties with programmatic data and site. Every stage is the diagram of the next stage. Every diagram darkens the stage before. It focuses everything in front of it, it blurs everything behind it. If you have found structural properties, there is no need to keep the diagram of the animation (third stage); it doesn't make sense. The structure is important now, not its features. Now you know your nodes and splittings, bendings and scalings, etc, ***that*** becomes the diagram to bring to the new level. No longer paper but cardboard – a very subtle difference. What was structured by tension can now be fixed in form. First the site, an absolutely amazing moment: everybody starts printing the site on different scales and comparing these with their model. Then the program, even more amazing: look what happens when I move the word "eating" over your model (which has now anchored on the site), when I move the word "watching football" over it, or the word "parking." Then the images (will you use one or two large screens, or 100 small ones?). Hardly a typical stadium – more like "electro-parks" – no problem to imagine them built, no problem at all. No problem seeing action and perception return, every minute, every second in the present – no problem at all.

THE STATE OF THE ART

Bob Lang

Looking ahead, and trying to imagine what might be around the corner, is what we are trained to do as engineers. To look and deliver what is beyond the obvious is in many ways a measure of attainment. Armed with such instinct, it is intriguing to think about where architecture may take us and how best to deal with what lies ahead. By reason, taste or fashion, we see architecture constantly examining itself, leading to change. Change can be prompted by external forces, perhaps social or economic in origin, or can be self-generated; maybe the radical simply in search of something new. That this scrutiny continues is as important as it is inevitable. So it is with engineering. It is a sense of enquiry that prompts our search for the new. Where to begin is not obvious: crystal-ball gazing alone invites risk and can be dangerous, but over-rigorous planning can be too prescriptive and insensitive to change. Instead we need a sympathetic response which interprets the evidence of today, both real and intuitive. This basis for judgement has more in common its subject. A little history also helps.

Recent trends in architecture have pushed us, and we in turn have pushed architecture. The explicit forms of the so-called "High-Tech" era have raw vitality, typified by early examples such as the Pompidou Center and the Renault Factory. The spirit of such buildings is not easily, if ever, recreated, especially with such freshness and vigor. Though it might be perfected and is often parodied – the sinews may be ever thinner, the glass plates ever larger and the fixings yet more delicate – it is easy to exhaust the limited repertoire of such form. The large masonry constructions of religious and cathedral architecture were surely the "high-tech" structures of their day. By reducing material in buttresses and stretching the span of domes and arches, they are masterpieces of design and construction. Yet in an industry possessed by contradiction, how strange that these buildings are now occasionally quoted as references for the mass they possess. This is particularly the case in today's search for environmentally responsible buildings.

The world at large is reliant upon our industry to fulfil its social obligations and do its part in establishing an acceptable urban fabric. Constructing buildings that draw as little as possible on natural resources is only one part and has much to do with science and investment in research. Research must continue unabated. In our position as professionals we must demand it. It is the nutrition of progress and tomorrow's designs. Advances in the design of environmentally responsible buildings characterize the architecture of the past decade or so. Yet in the design of today's "green buildings," which must become as much a part of our life as reclaiming tin cans, a mono-form, often rectilinear and occasionally massive, is prevalent. It is a kind of refurbishment of traditional form with new gadgets, relying on various and diverse appendages to direct and block the elements. Yet the physical laws governing the dynamics of fluids, heat, sound, light, and force – which we seek to manipulate in our green buildings – are for the most part non-linear. While growth and decay are described by curves, we are constrained within a rectilinear straitjacket. It is little wonder our buildings often appear festooned with devices. A comparison with car design is valuable. Look at the recent changes in car body profiles. In the quest for an improved drag coefficient, smooth, curved forms now acknowledge and manage fluid flow. If only on the grounds of aesthetics, scrutiny is sure to land on today's green architecture. The search will be, already is, on for something new, but what and where next?

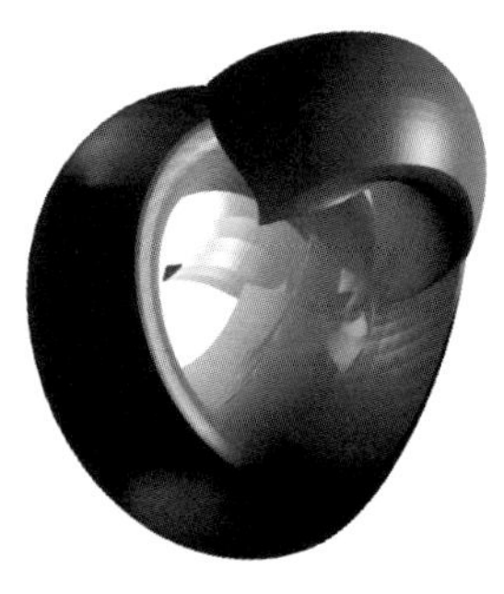

Engineers can continue to imagine, or perhaps architecture might lead us. As a profession bridging both art and science, we might search for clues in mathematics and physics. During this century, across the sciences, reductionist thinking has been challenged. Quantum mechanics and later breakthroughs in non-linear mathematics have confirmed that we will not see the whole picture by just studying its individual pans in isolation. A system can be more than the sum of its parts. Loosely, a non-linear system cannot be represented adequately by simply adding individual results. In structural engineering terms, superposition does not apply. Gaudi's chains are one example. Further afield, anecdote has it that meteorologists were much maligned in the late 1950s when they first confronted reductionist thinking. In investigating "in full" the weather system – with the aid of their new electronic computers – they found order and patterns within a seemingly chaotic and unpredictable system. They chose to investigate complex order to solve their problems. This order could only be revealed by rapid and repeated calculation. Today, whole university departments are dedicated to extending their ideas. To consider a revolution of non-reductionist thinking in engineering or architecture is interesting. Would it create something new or merely install acceptance of some of the more abstract and experimental forms on the fringes of today's architecture? What would it produce? A less obvious order? Double curvature? Abstract form? The opportunity to re-visit natural forms? It can be argued that buildings offered as apparently abstract, non-linear geometries are solely reactionist, even antagonistic. Each can be seen as just an exercise in sculpture. Fine, why not? On cultural grounds alone such experiment is necessary. But if seeing them in this way provides an excuse to reject all such forms we should think again. If we are looking to optimize the physical properties of our buildings, then some of the most responsive forms which result might appear equally obscure. They could be jagged-straight or doubly-curved, perhaps a bit of both. They may be transitional or abrupt. Accepting and not reducing. Derived geometry in response to some non-linear input. The examples of the hanging chain structures of Gaudi and Otto have their equivalents using the stimulus of heat, light and sound. Curved and non-linear geometry is as yet untapped in architecture as a generator of seriously derived forms.

Taking advantage of this might require us to re-evaluate our concept of surface and maybe space. We should be looking towards the mathematics of surface definition, now widespread in three-dimensional-modeling computer programs. We need to consider how this technology will transfer to, and influence, construction. In sculptural terms, the new museum in Bilbao took the first tentative steps on this road, but a whole journey remains. Remember that the computing power that permitted the meteorologists to revolutionize their thinking probably sits comfortably in a brief case today.

Today we can analyze and predict the performance of shell-like surface structures to a degree where the analysis begins to outstrip practice. The method of construction and the tolerances which are achievable become paramount. In these circumstances collaboration is necessary to allow the designer and builder to iterate and progress. We need a circular process of refinement with the lead constantly changing, but the diverse motives of our disparate industry often prevents this. To introduce these new geometries as serious concepts requires industry-wide acceptance of open collaboration. This is not easy when closed competition is often interpreted as the only way to achieve value. But change is coming Bureaucratic-sounding, jargon-ridden concepts such as "win-win" and "partnering" have at their core a desire to collaborate; and the recognition that the earlier this collaboration occurs, the better. A spirit such as this is essential. In an industry still paralleling itself with the mass-production doctrine of early this century, we must progress beyond a reductionist, self similar, Meccano mentality. Our procurement methods have to be rearranged to allow this to happen, just as the methods by which we cost our buildings have to acknowledge construction methodology and not rely on magical rates that encompass all. For too long we have stood by and let our industry fragment, and erect protected enclaves that limit consultation and result in a game of pass the parcel. We might now be hampering progress. Gaining the acceptance of new forms and geometries serves to crystallize how we might take our industry forward. The co-operation engendered will advance us beyond our reductionist system of procurement. That we opened this discussion in search of new form and concluded with commentary on procurement is not mis-guided or lacking direction. Rather it is the manifestation of the complex system that is construction. A tour that shows change in one area is unlikely be perfected without a different scale of impact elsewhere. So, issues surrounding the search for the new will extend to each and every aspect of our business. Such re-examination cannot be avoided and, as said earlier, that it continues is as important as it is inevitable.

[destadium]³

Gianfranco Bombaci (I)
Pieter Lozie (B)

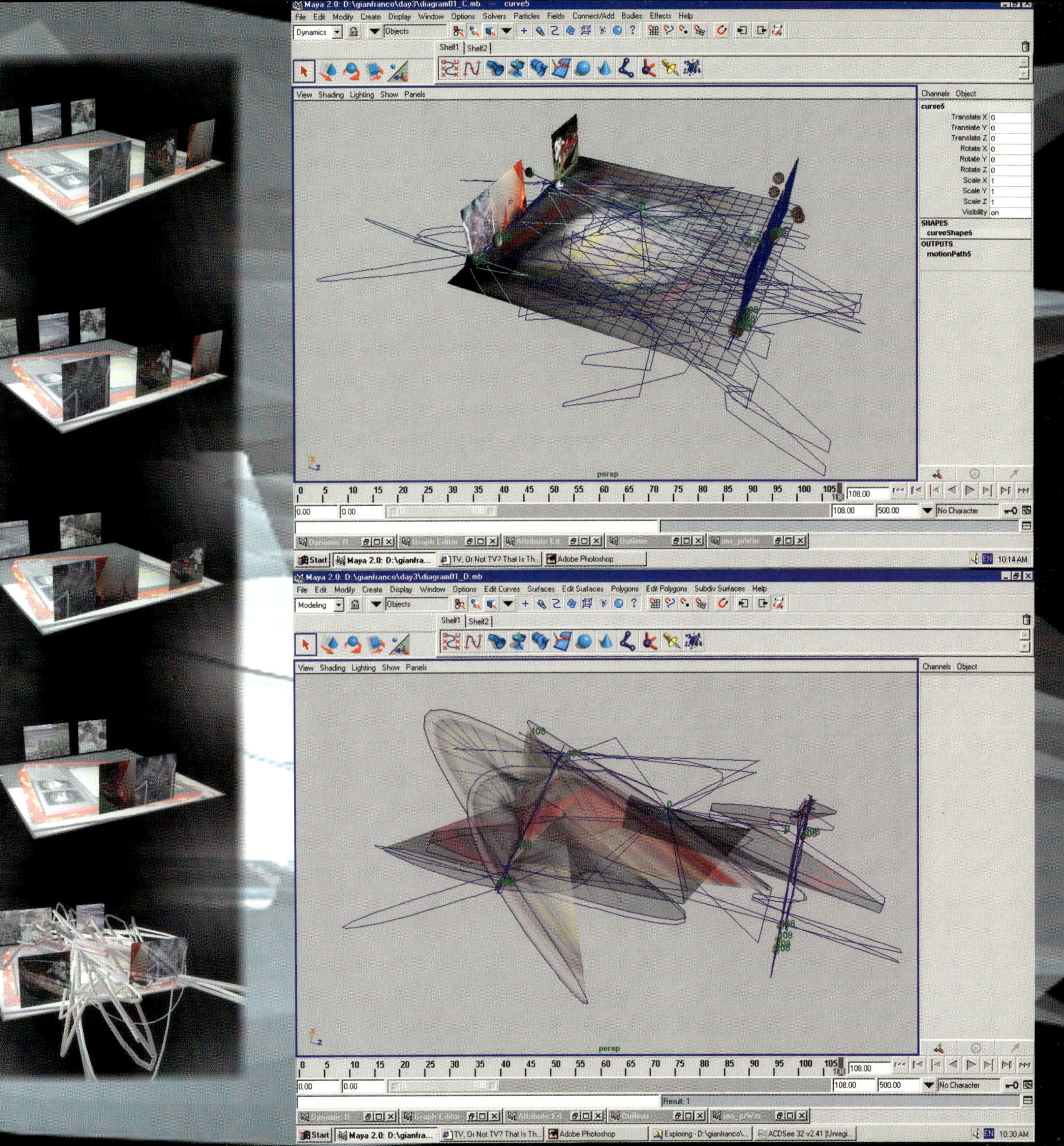

Maya 2.0: D:\gianfranco\day3\diagram01_C.mb --- curve5
File Edit Modify Create Display Window Options Solvers Particles Fields Connect/Add Bodies Effects Help
Dynamics
Objects
Shelf1 Shelf2
View Shading Lighting Show Panels
Channels Object
curve5
Translate X 0
Translate Y 0
Translate Z 0
Rotate X 0
Rotate Y 0
Rotate Z 0
Scale X 1
Scale Y 1
Scale Z 1
Visibility on
SHAPES
curveShape5
OUTPUTS
motionPath5
persp
108.00
500.00
No Character
Start
Maya 2.0: D:\gianfra...
TV, Or Not TV? That Is Th...
Adobe Photoshop
10:14 AM
Maya 2.0: D:\gianfranco\day3\diagram01_D.mb
File Edit Modify Create Display Window Options Edit Curves Surfaces Edit Surfaces Polygons Edit Polygons Subdiv Surfaces Help
Modeling
Objects
Shelf1 Shelf2
View Shading Lighting Show Panels
Channels Object
persp
108.00
500.00
No Character
Result: 1
Start
Maya 2.0: D:\gianfra...
TV, Or Not TV? That Is Th...
Adobe Photoshop
Exploring - D:\gianfranco\...
ACDSee 32 v2.41 [Unregi...
10:30 AM

CAVE

Markus Randler (D)
Angelo Grasso (I)

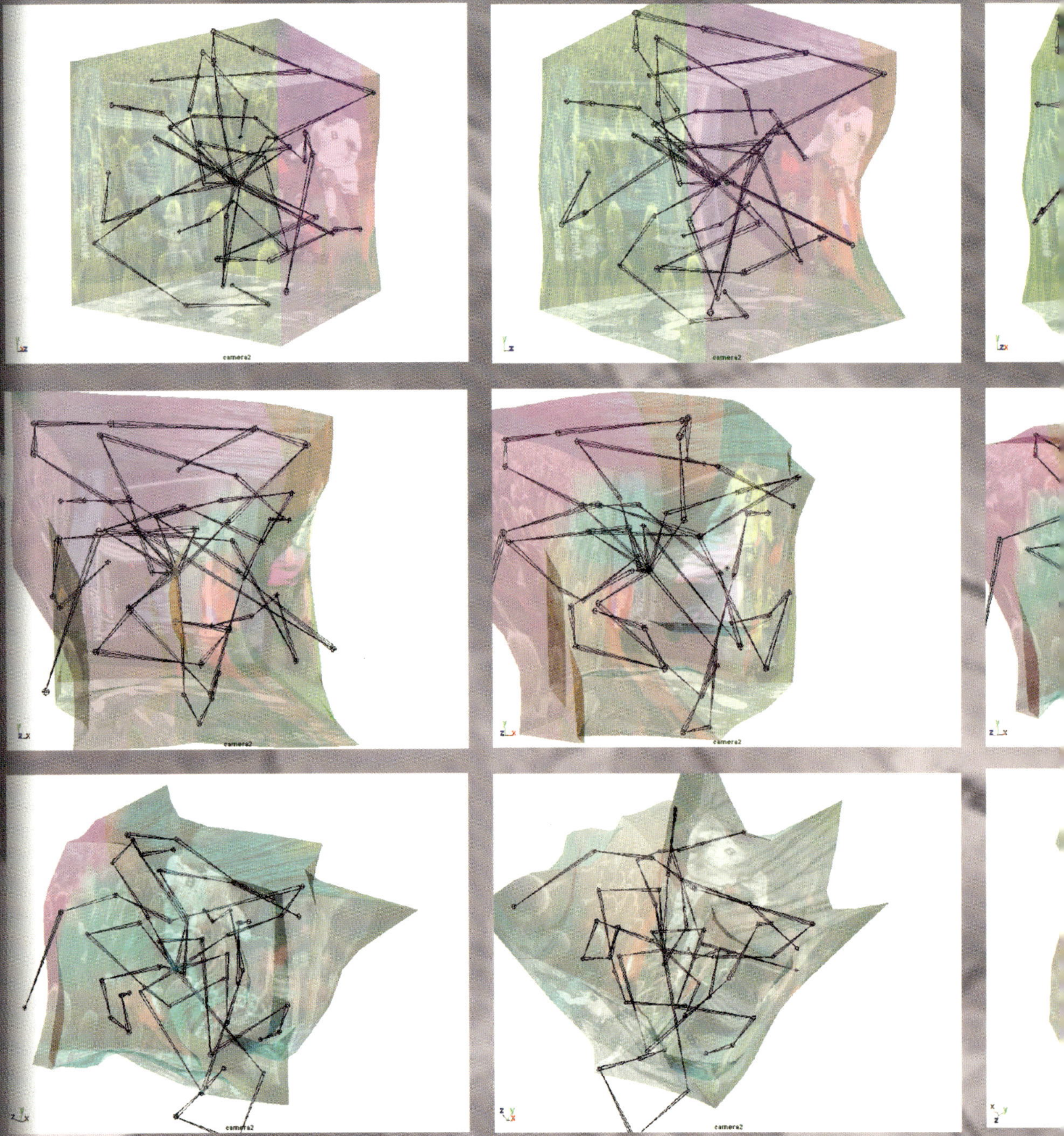

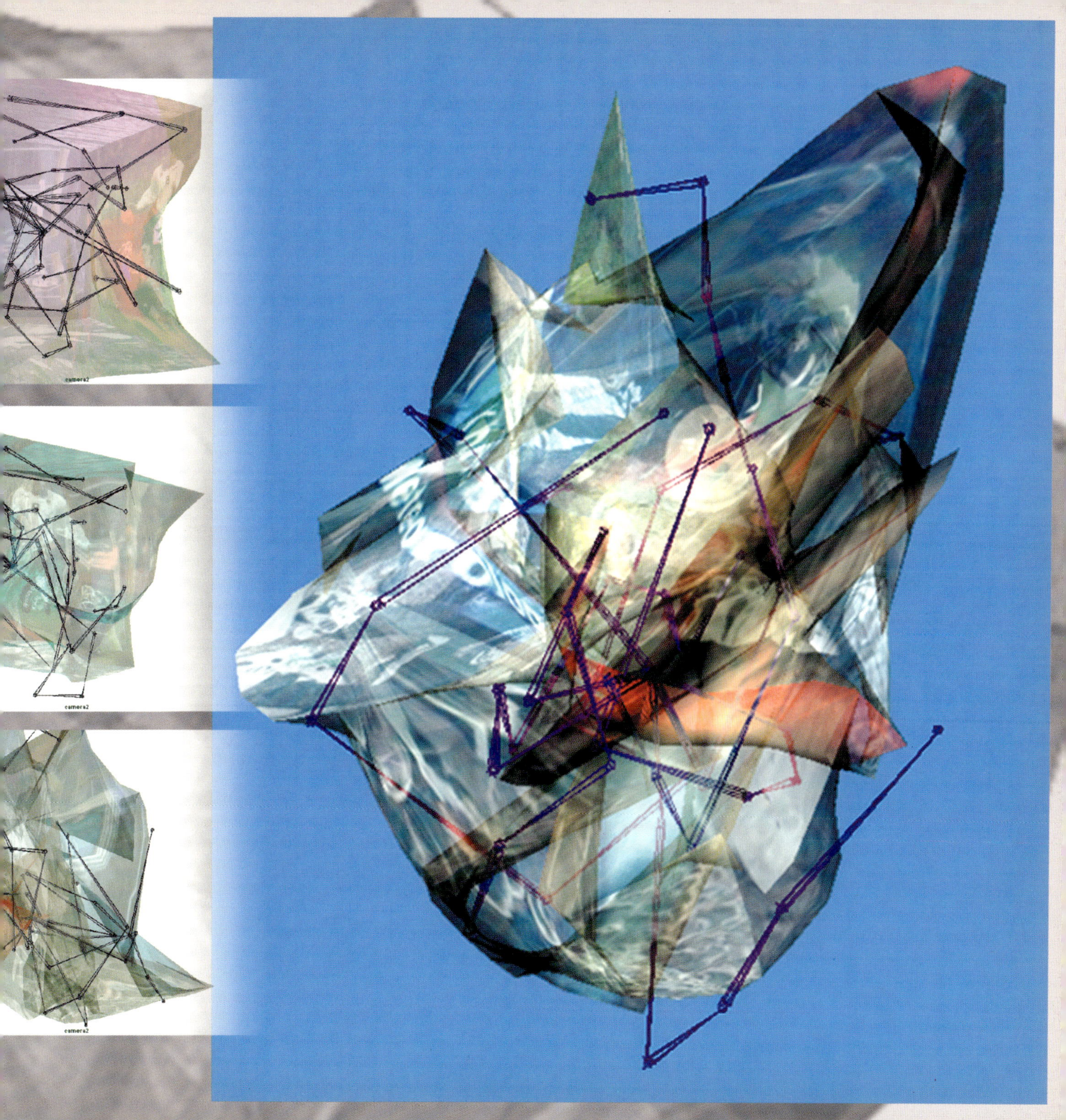
camera2
camera2
camera2

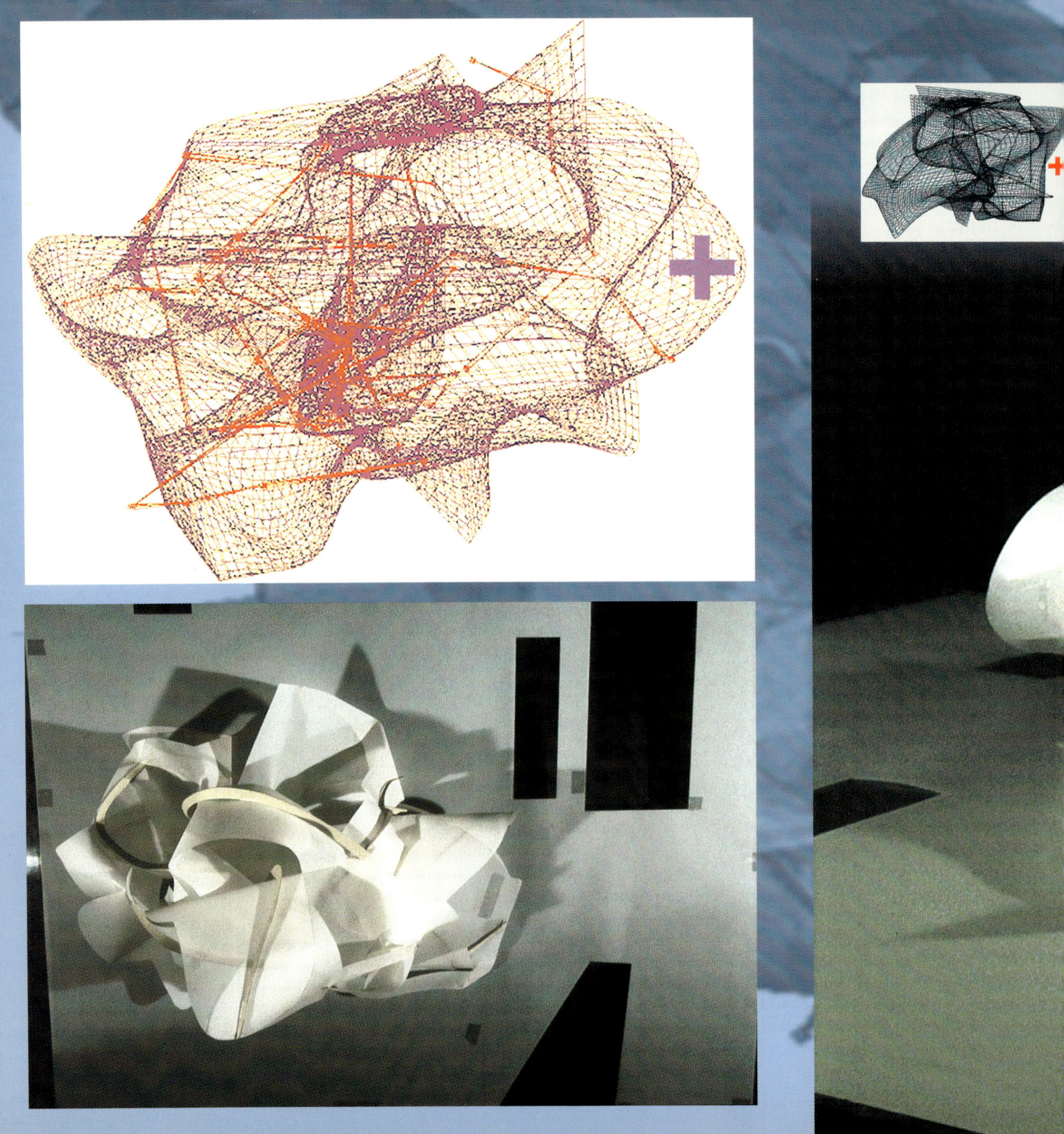

90 MIN
Fabian Wallmüller (A)
Dirk Weiblen (D)
ball
audience
player1
player2
playfield
source
analyze
programing
transforming
break
player b
goal2
ball
spectators
player a
goal1
eventtime
90 min
soccer universe
fabian wallmuller
dirk weiblen 8-99

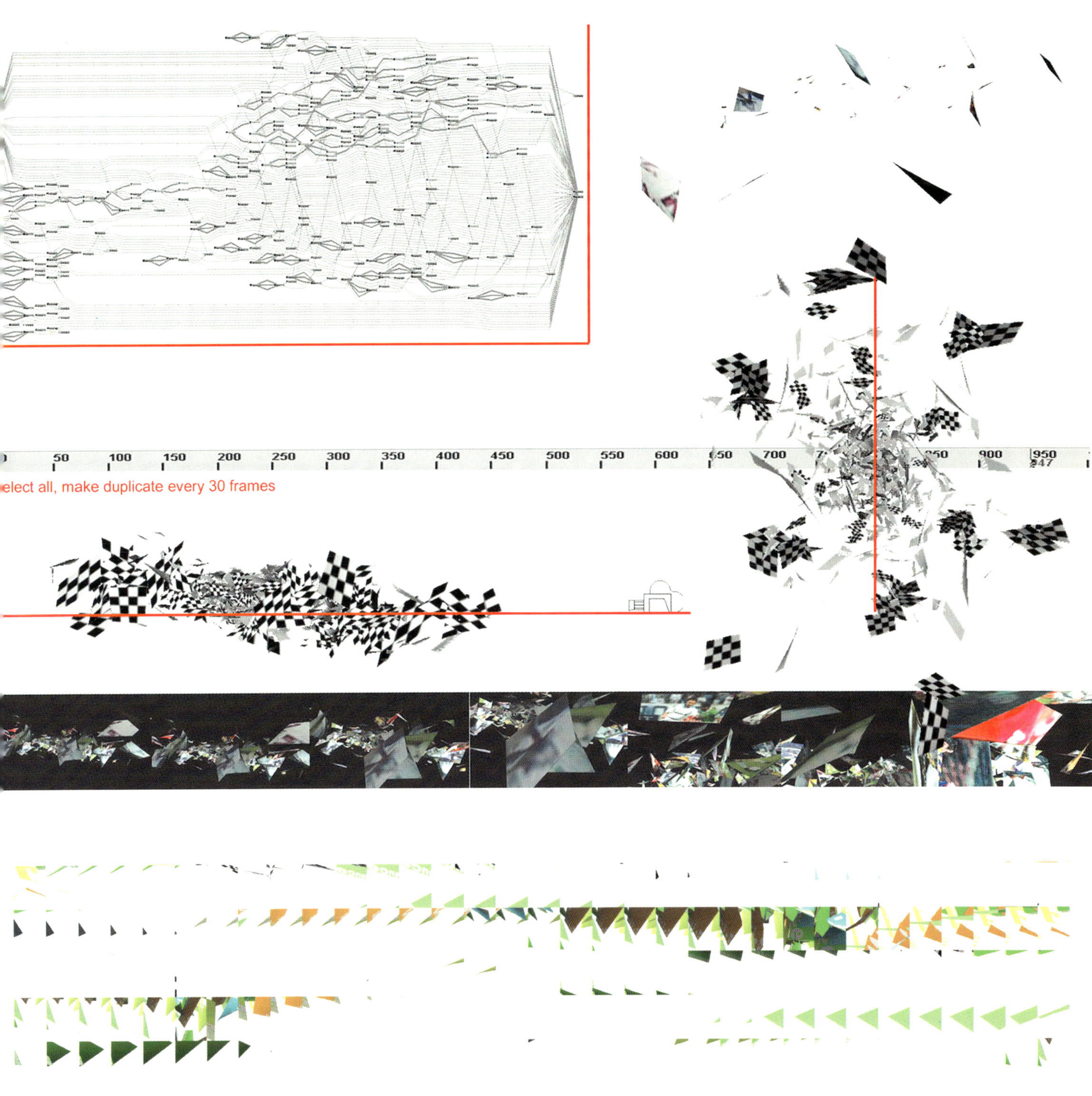

50 100 150 200 250 300 350 400 450 500 550 600 650 700 850 900 950
elect all, make duplicate every 30 frames

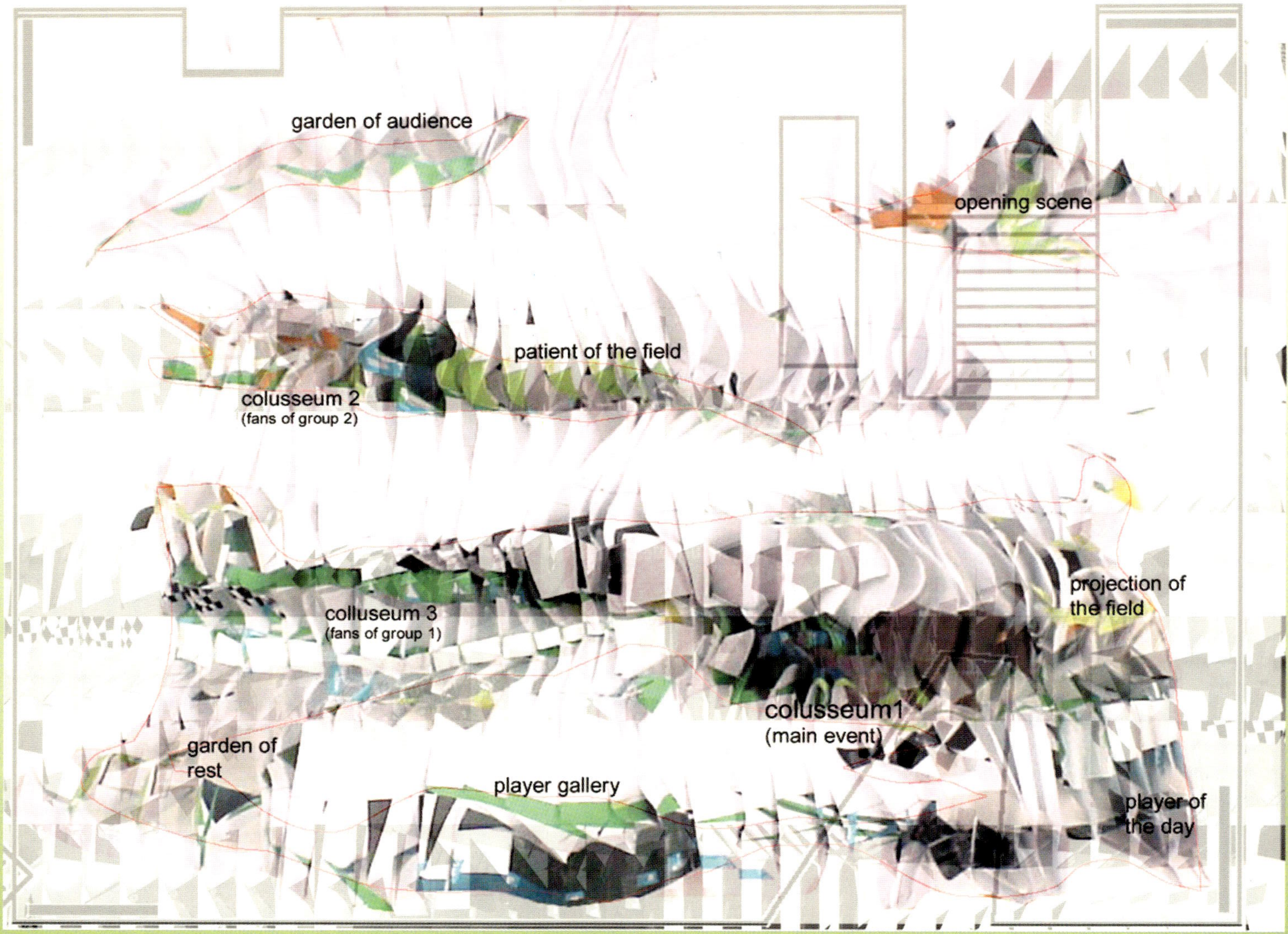

garden of audience
opening scene
patient of the field
colusseum 2
(fans of group 2)
projection of the field
colluseum 3
(fans of group 1)
colusseum1
(main event)
garden of rest
player gallery
player of the day

Florian Wicke (A)
Craig Chatman (AUS)
SOFTBALL

PAPER
READING STRUCTURE
NAi
THE NETHERLANDS
ARCHITECTURE INSTITUTE
LARS SPUYBROEK & BOB LANG
THE WEIGHT OF THE IMAGE
V2_Lab

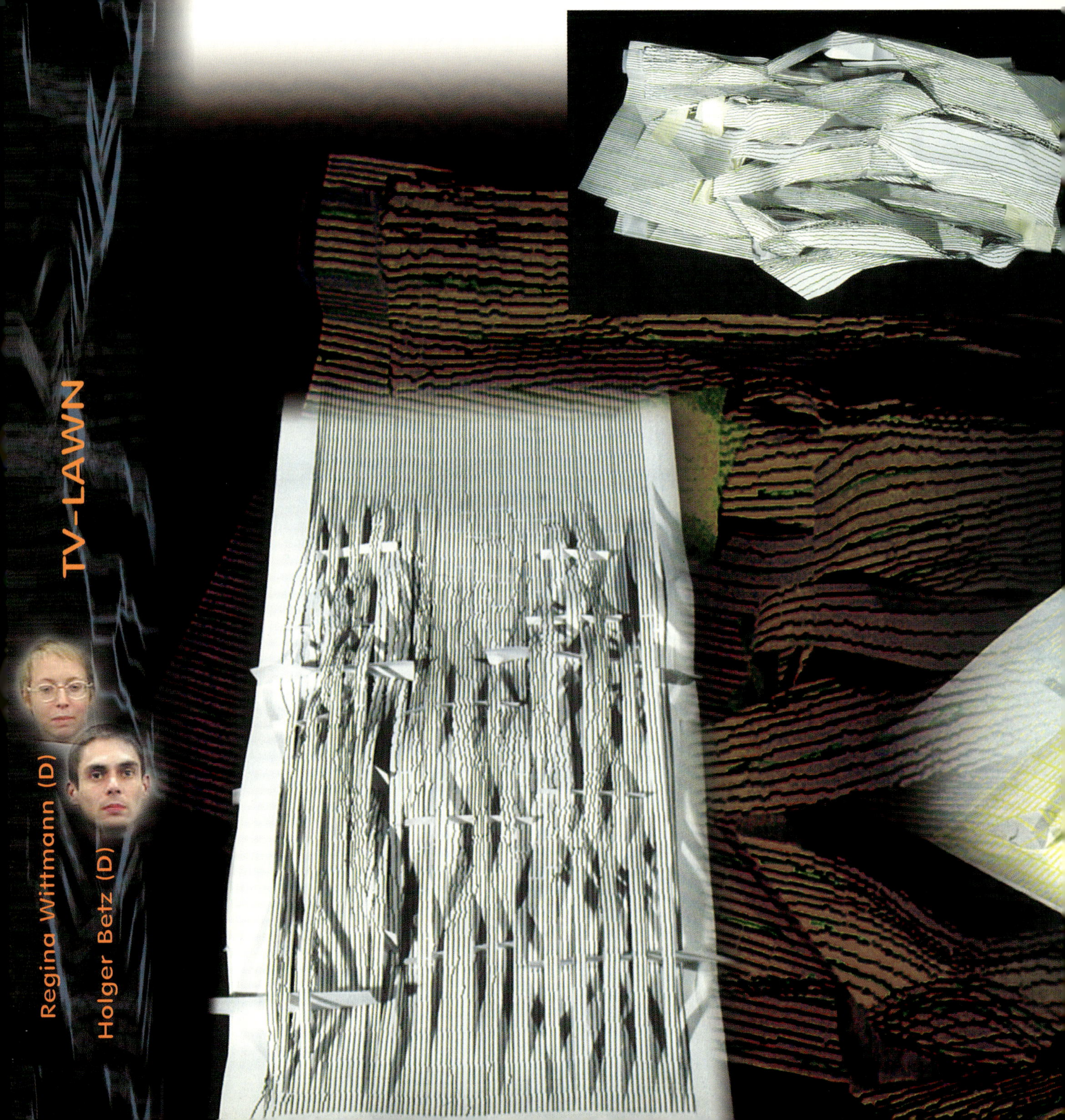
TV-LAWN
Regina Wittmann (D)
Holger Betz (D)

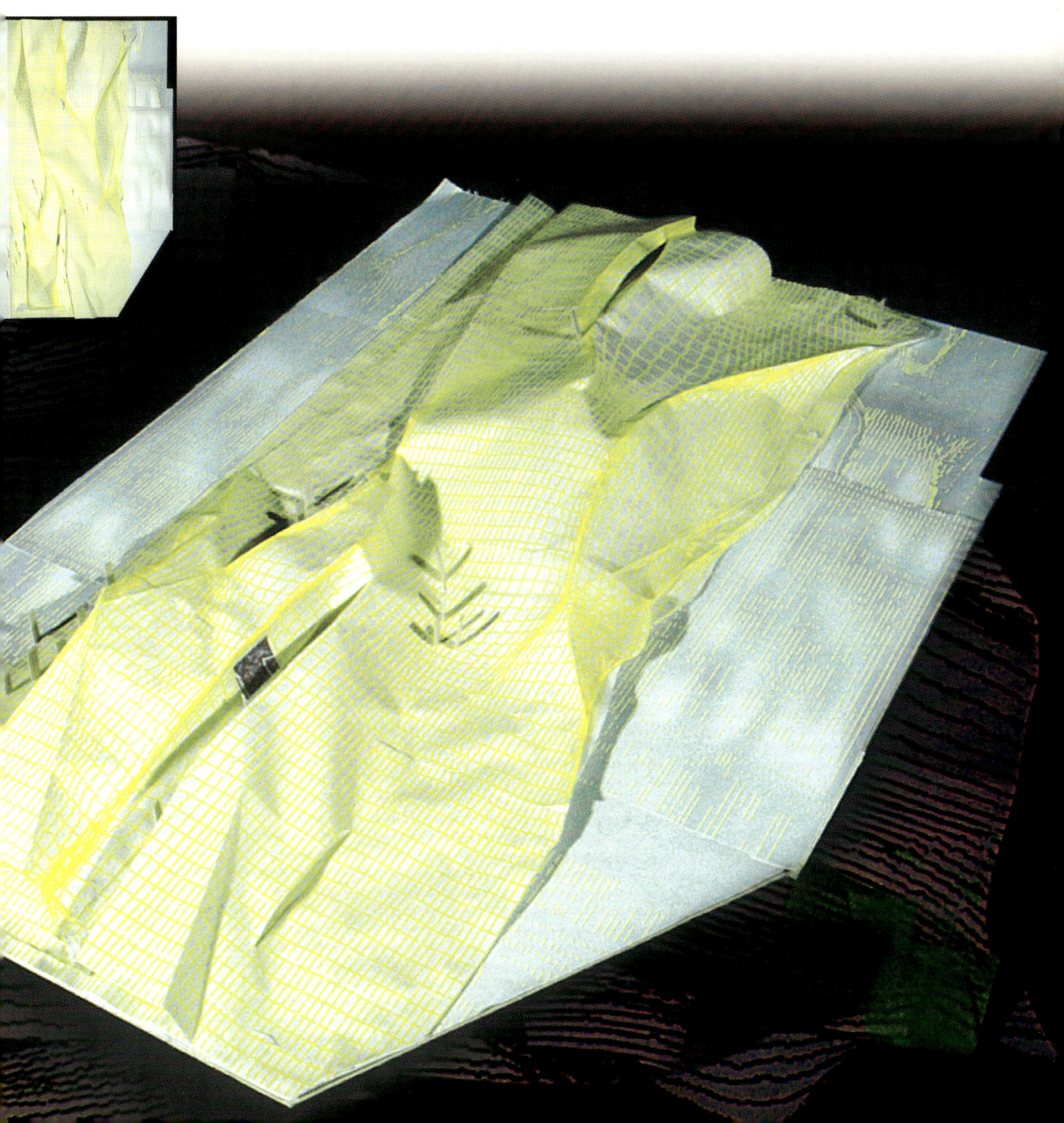

SPORT-BARS
Joshua Stein (USA)
Iris Karminski (A)

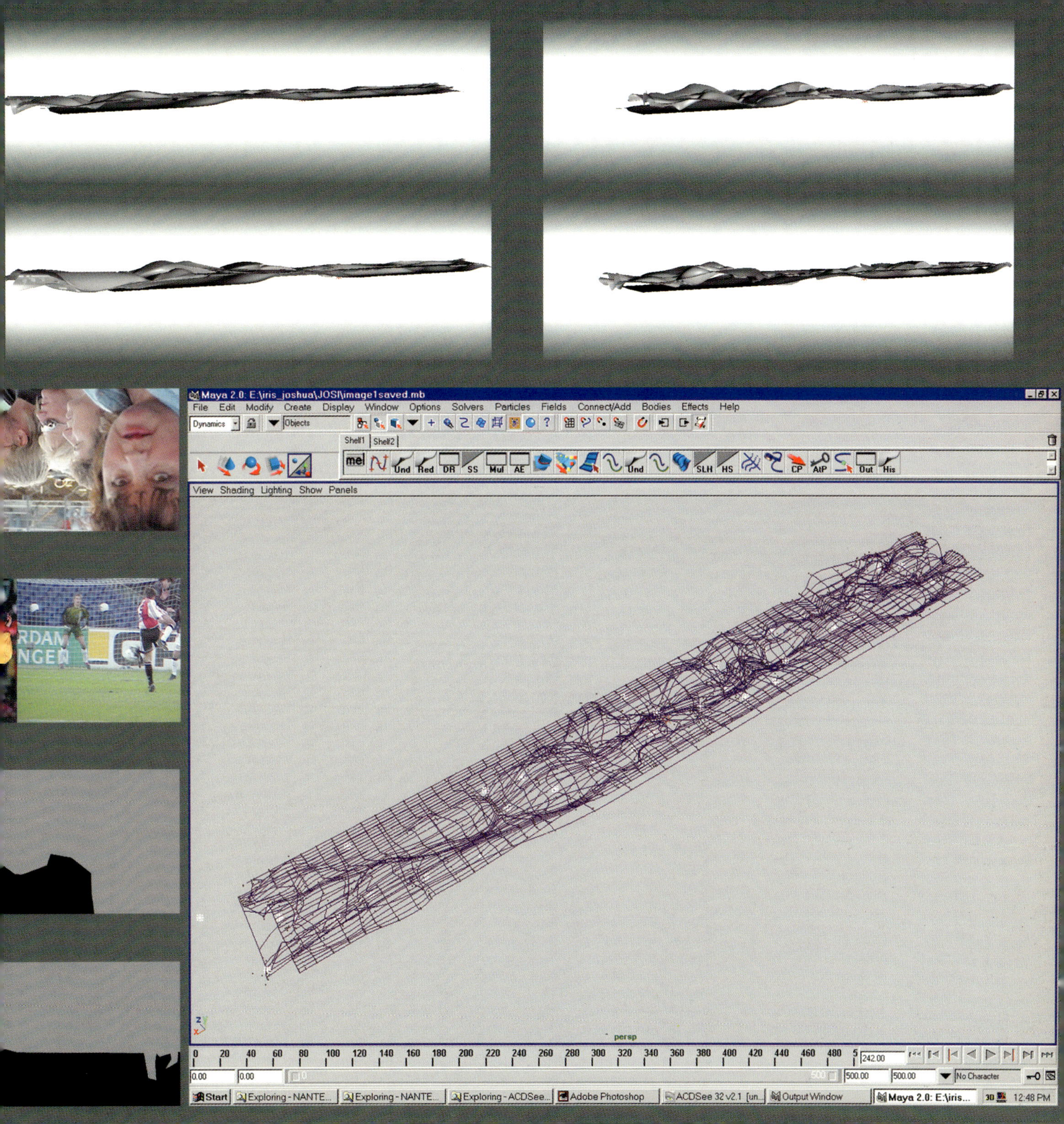

Maya 2.0: E:\iris_joshua\JOSI\image1saved.mb
File Edit Modify Create Display Window Options Solvers Particles Fields Connect/Add Bodies Effects Help
Dynamics
Objects
Shell1 Shell2
mel
Und Red DR SS Mul AE Und SLH HS CP AtP Out His
View Shading Lighting Show Panels
persp
0 20 40 60 80 100 120 140 160 180 200 220 240 260 280 300 320 340 360 380 400 420 440 460 480
242.00
0.00 0.00 500.00 500.00
No Character
Start
Exploring - NANTE...
Exploring - NANTE...
Exploring - ACDSee...
Adobe Photoshop
ACDSee 32 v2.1 [un...
Output Window
Maya 2.0: E:\iris...
12:48 PM

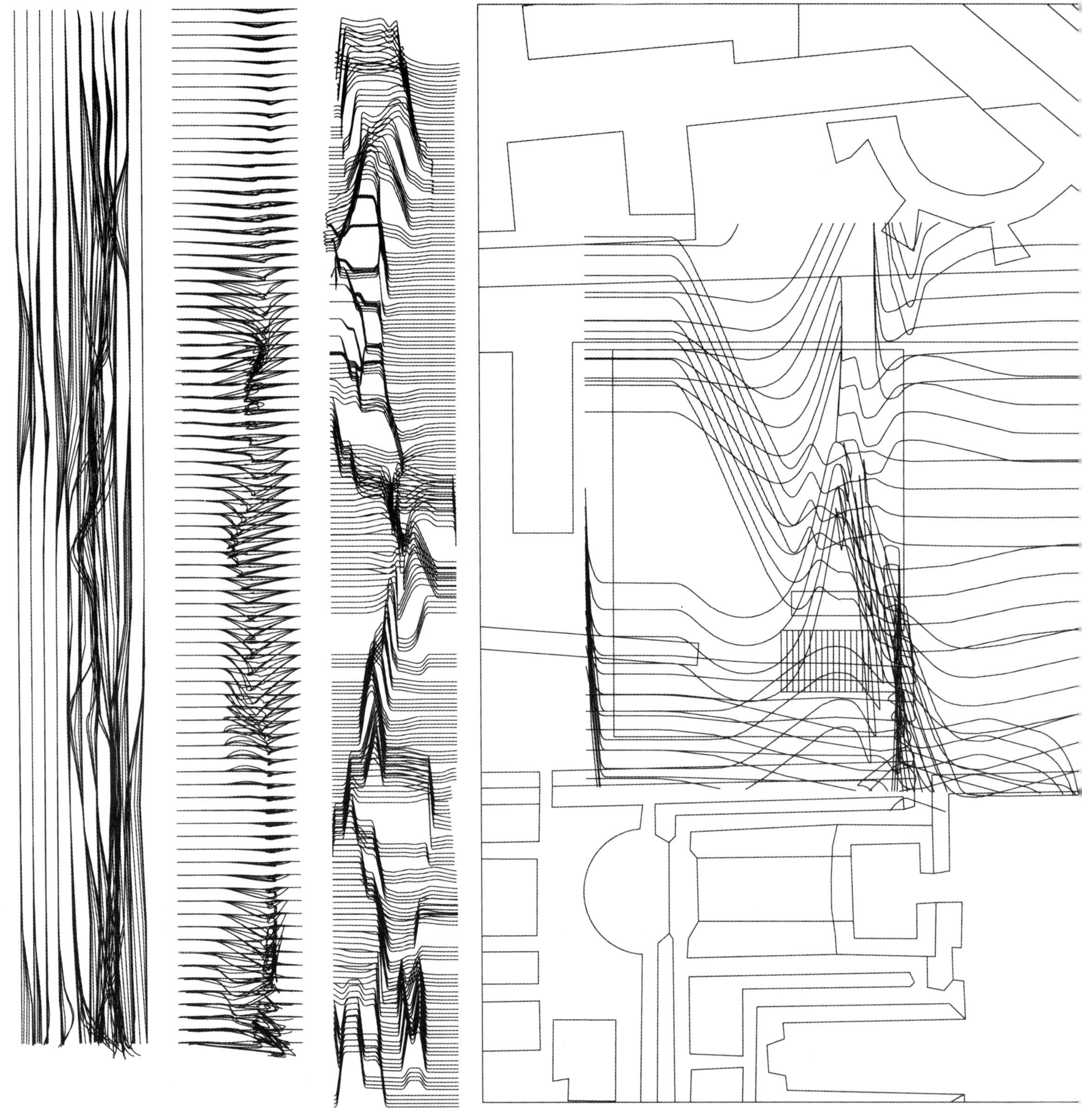

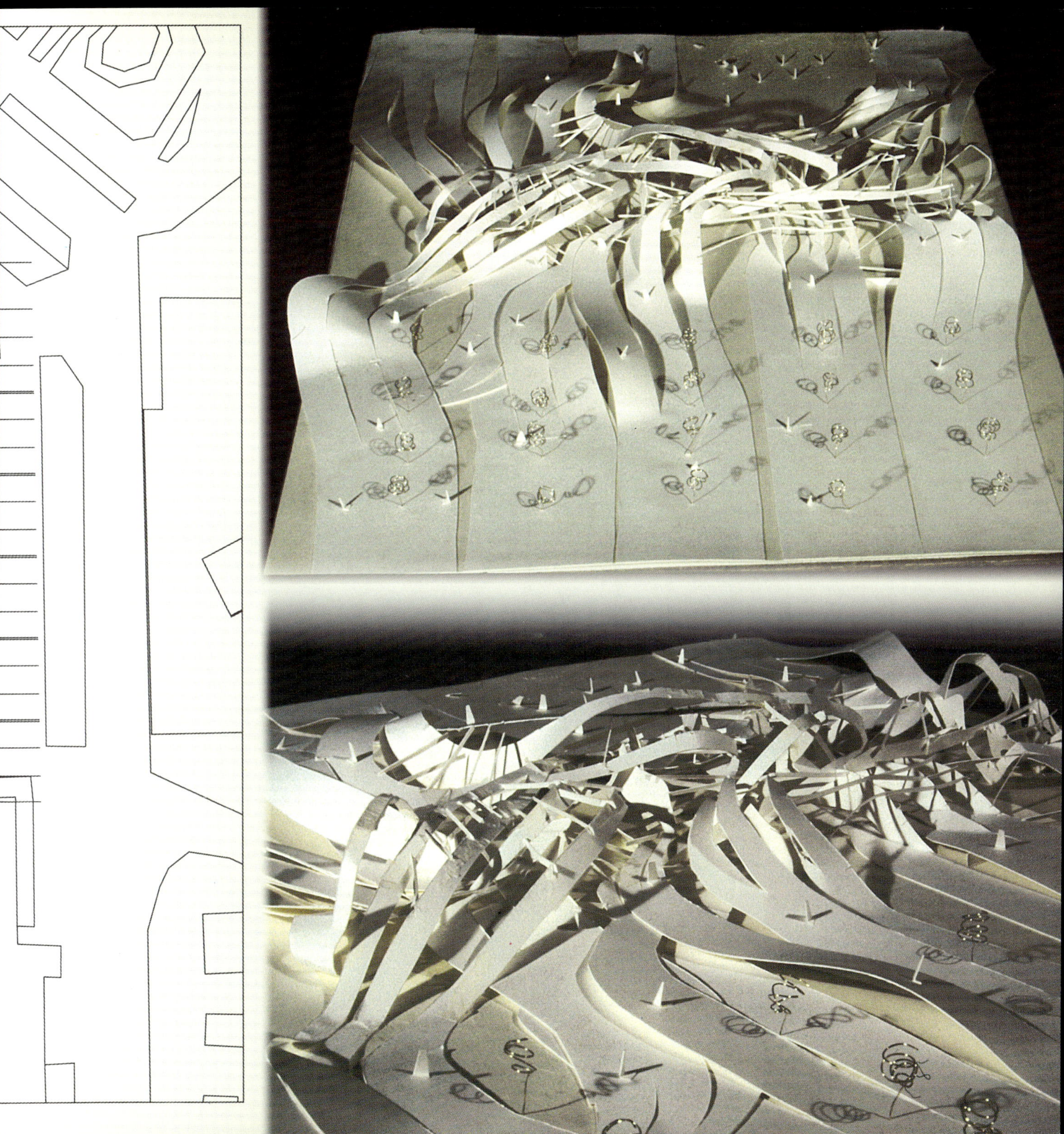

SMOKE
Yusuf Erbug Bengüler (TR)
Jochen Baumgartner (A)

SMOKE
NAI MASTERCLASS 1999
JOCHEN BAUMGARTNER, YUSUF ERBUG

THE ORGONE BOX

Oliver Tessmann (D)
Andrew Thurlow (USA)

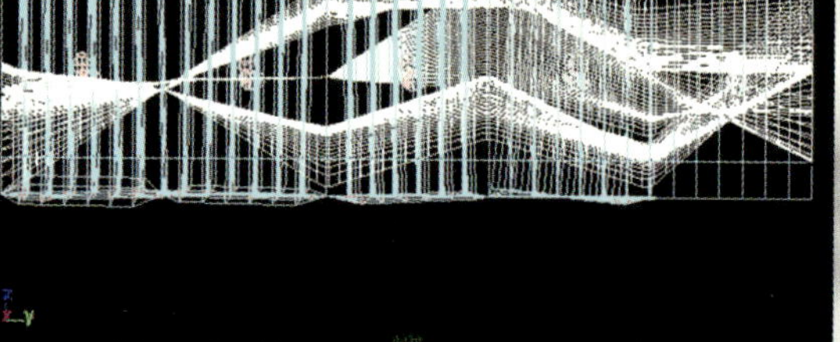
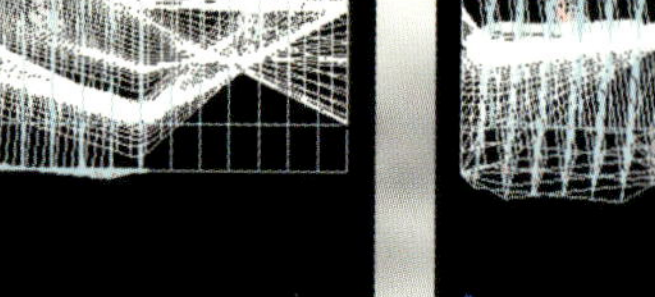
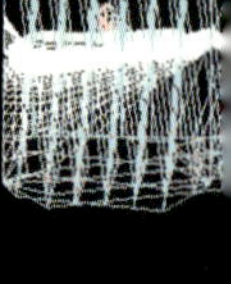
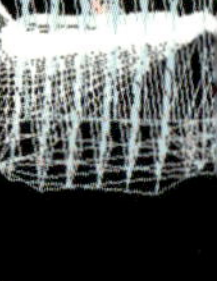

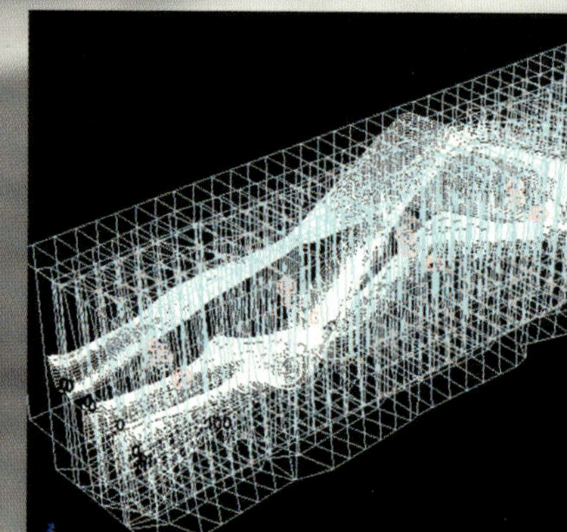
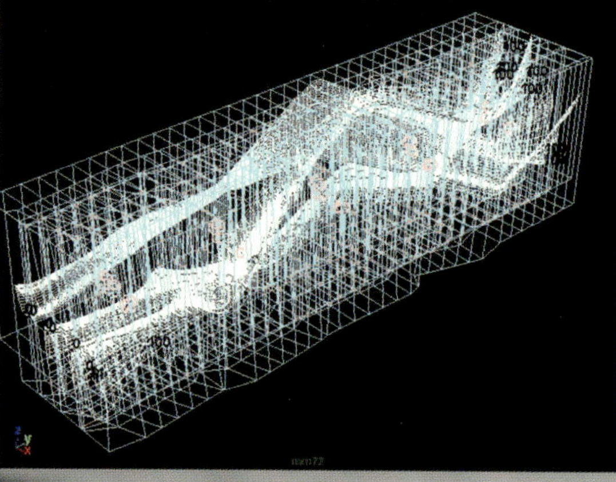
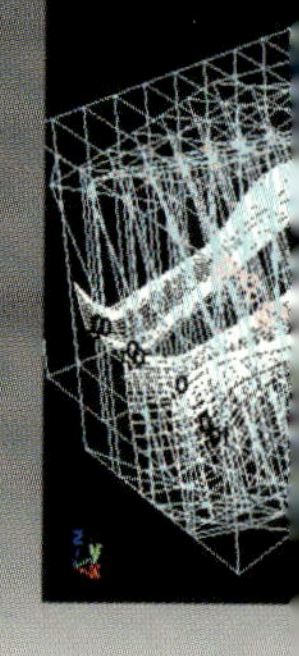

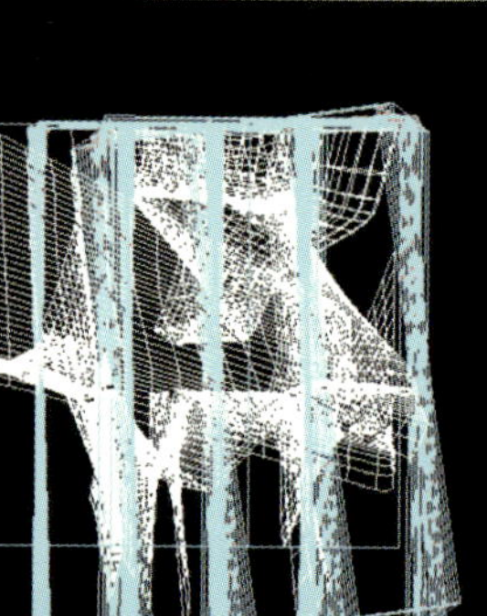

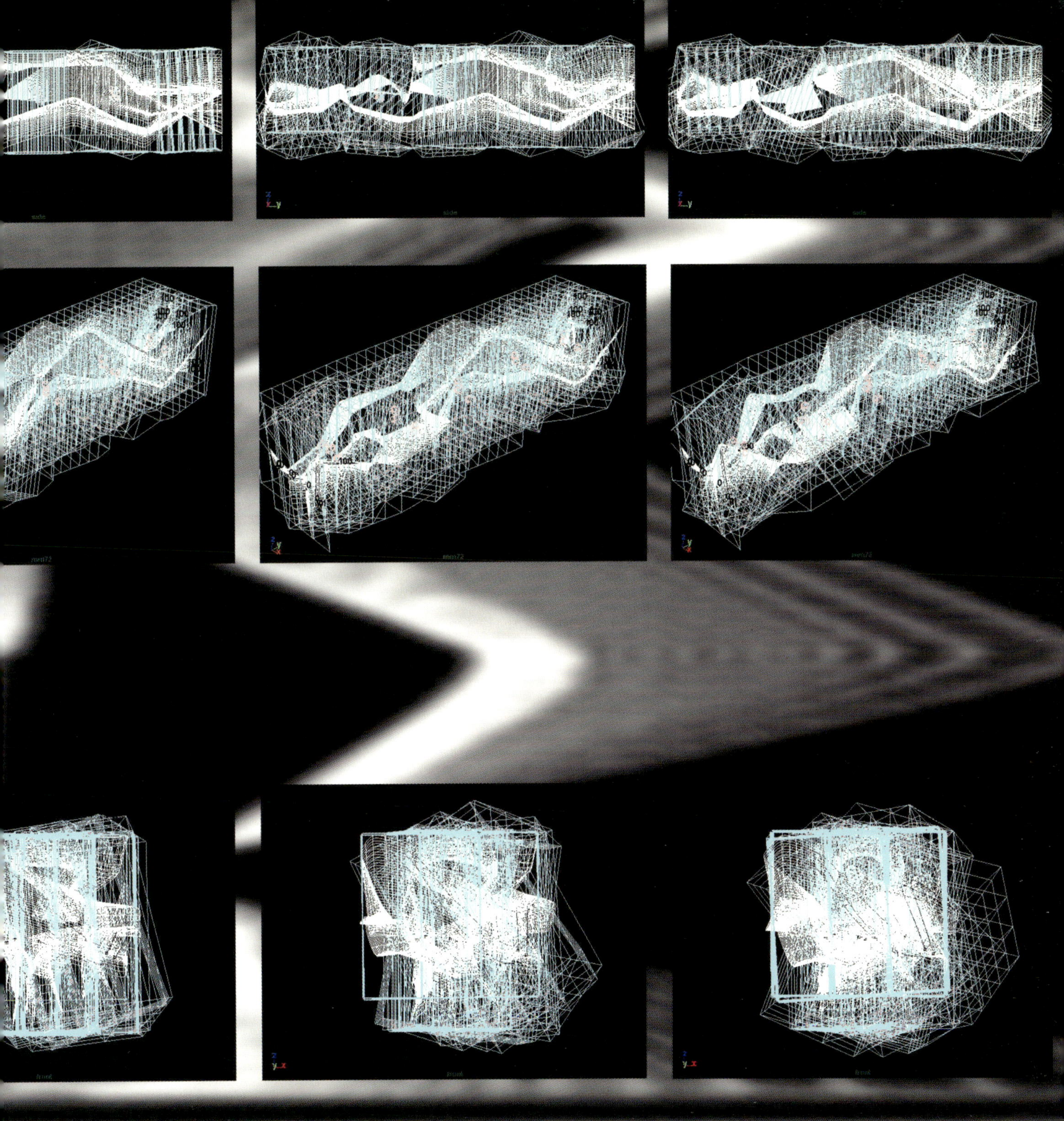

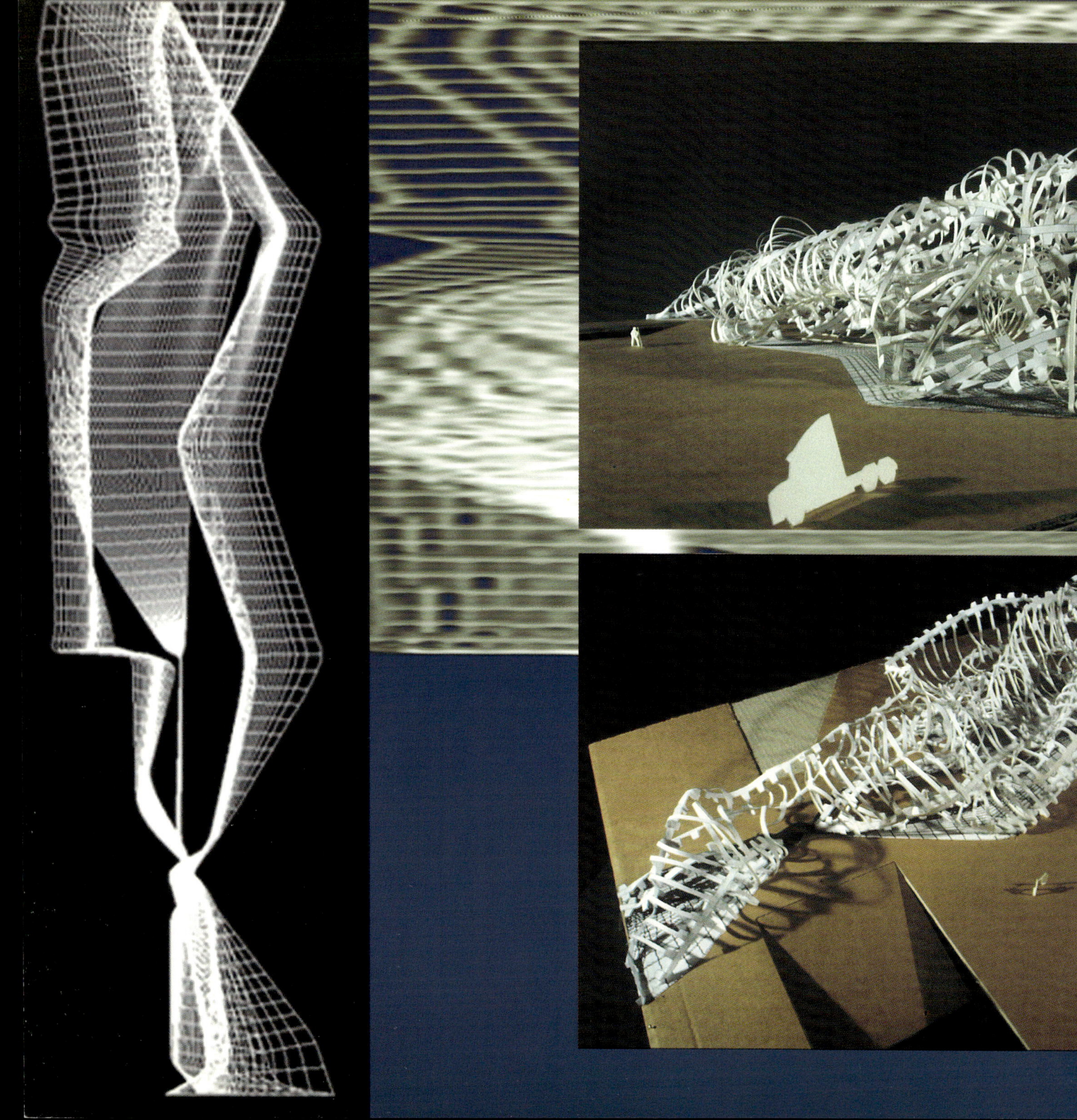

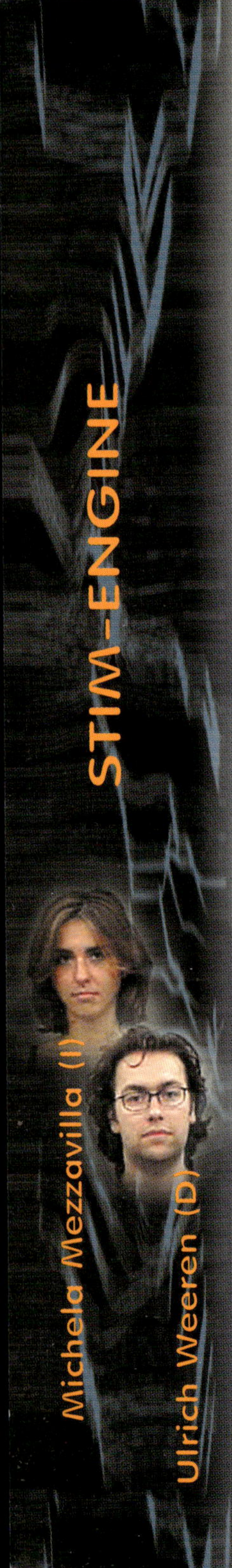

structure of the game

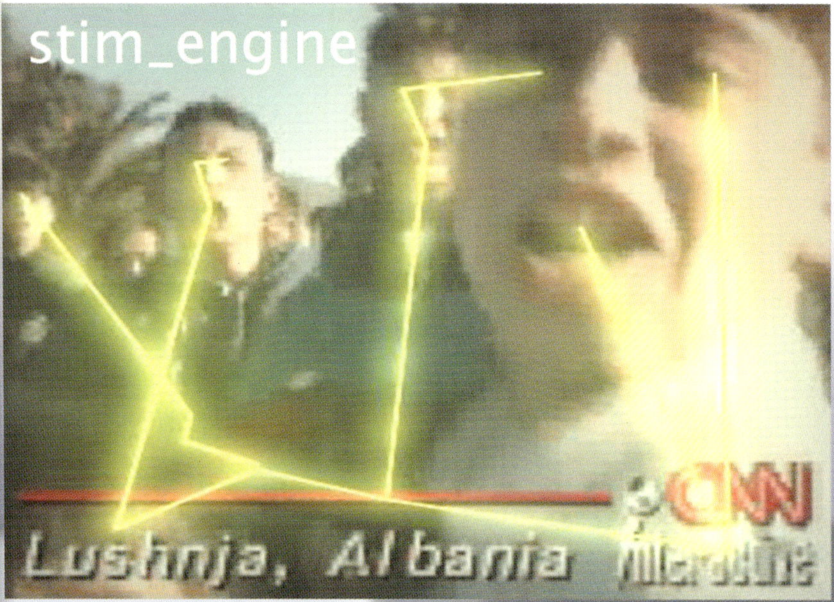

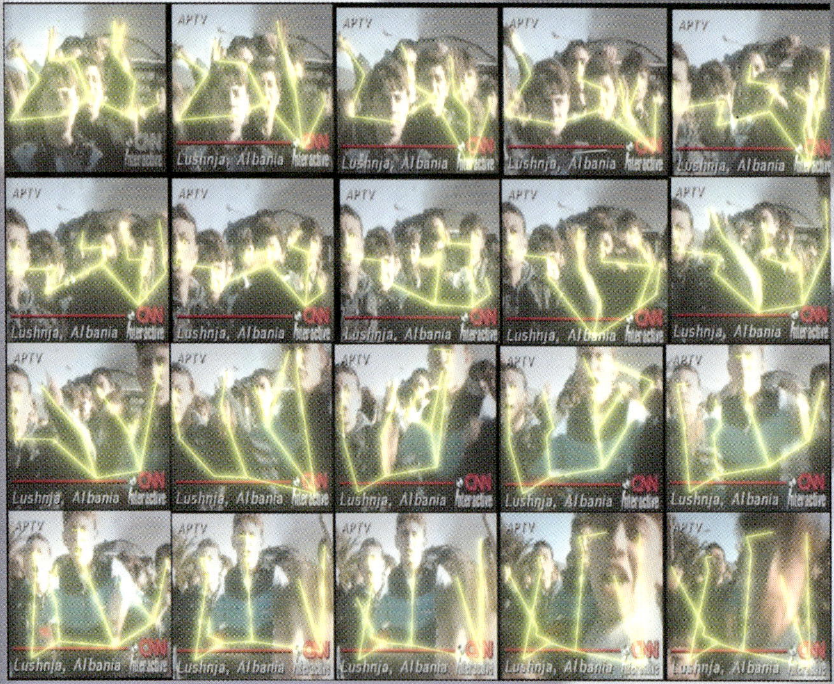

stim_engine

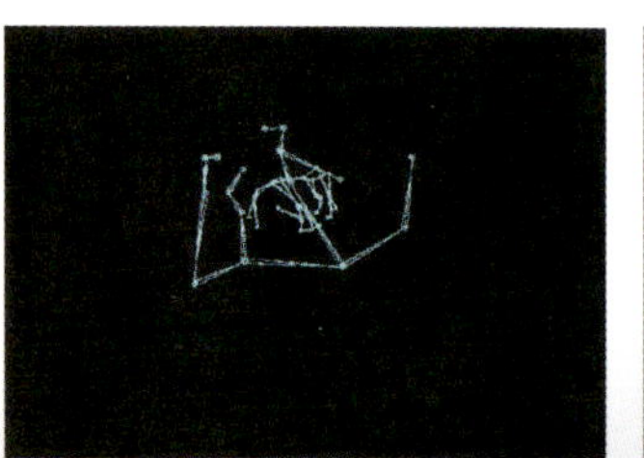

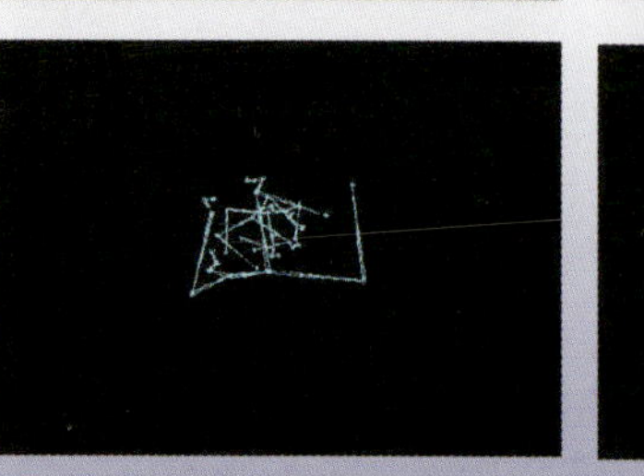

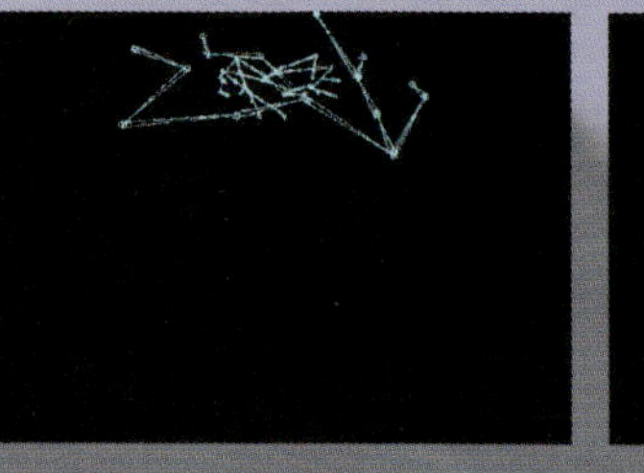

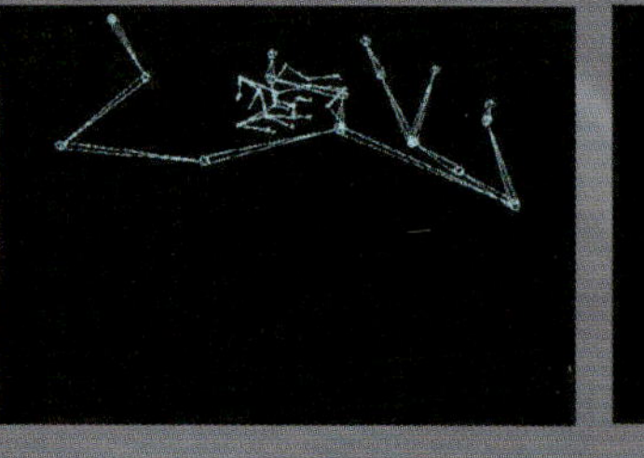

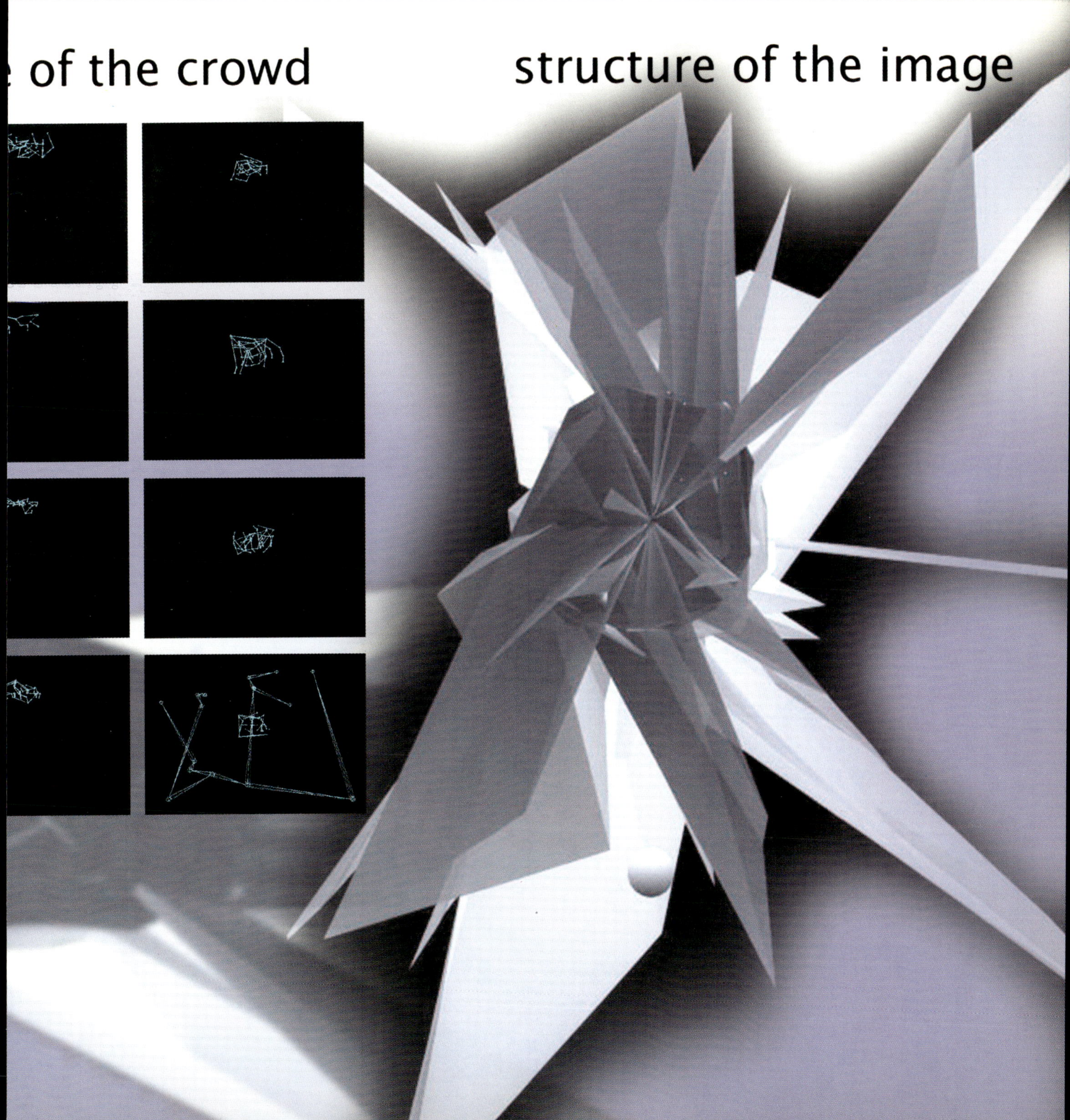
of the crowd
structure of the image

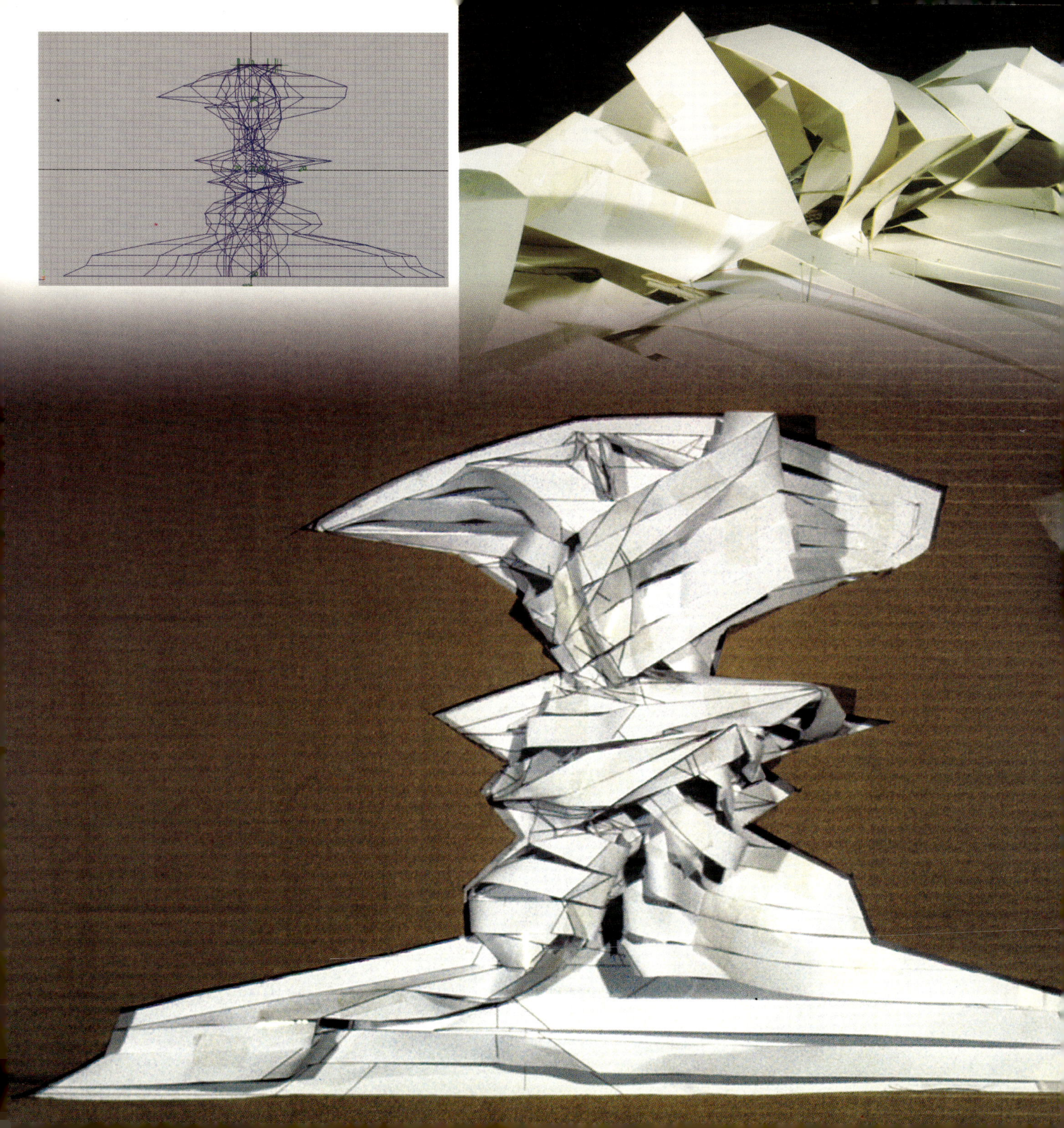

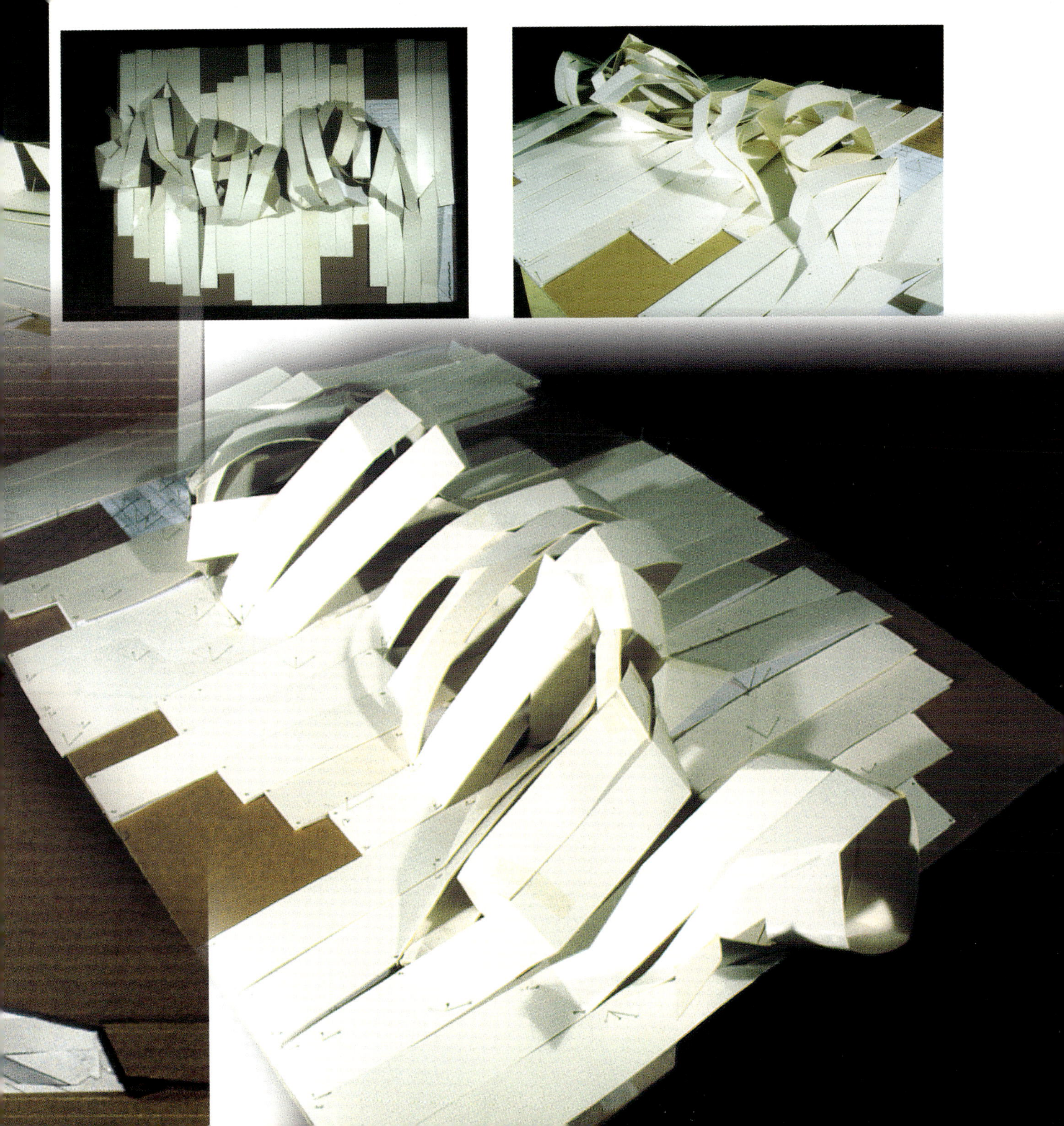

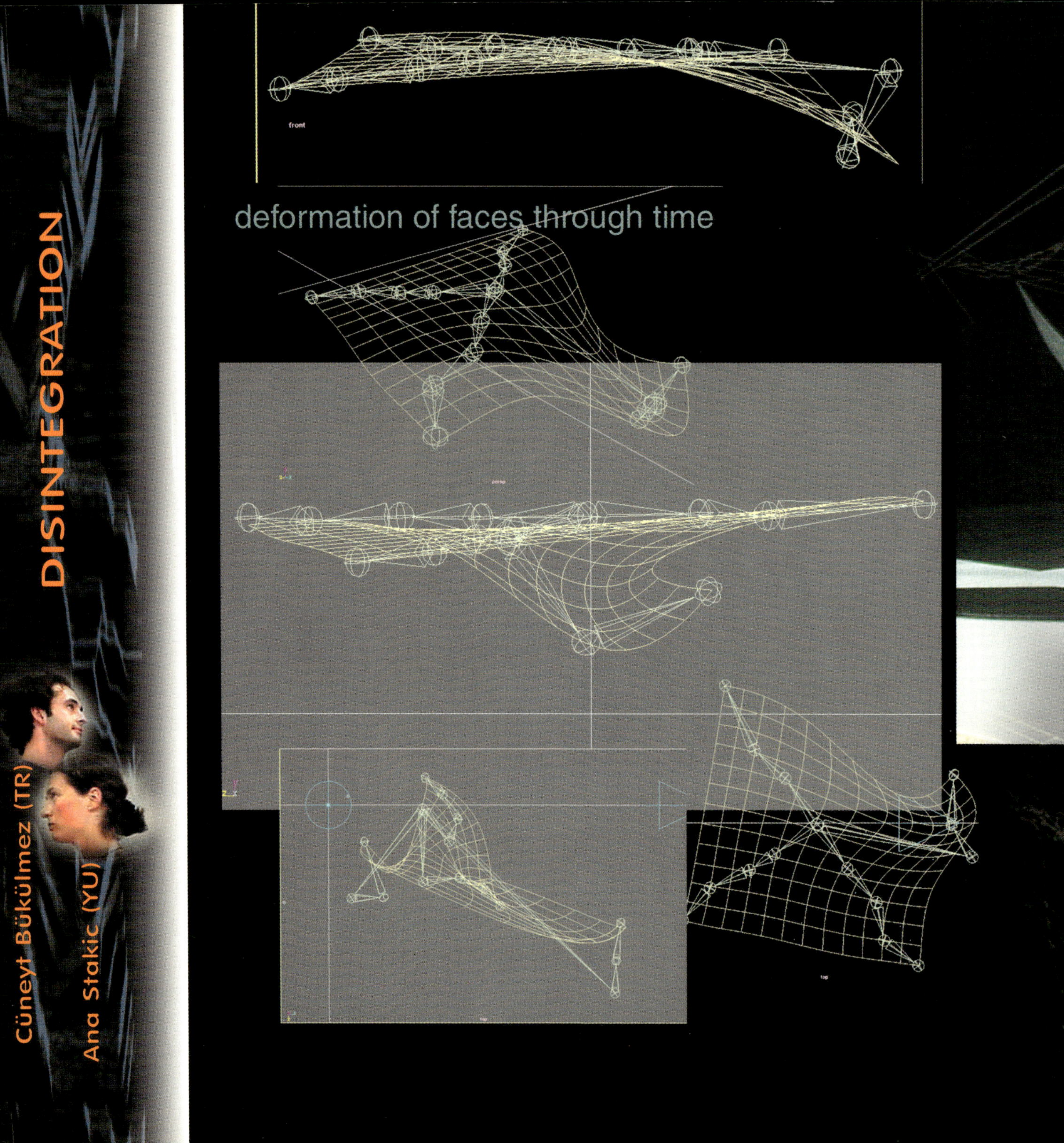
DISINTEGRATION
Cüneyt Bükülmez (TR)
Ana Stakic (YU)
deformation of faces through time
front
top

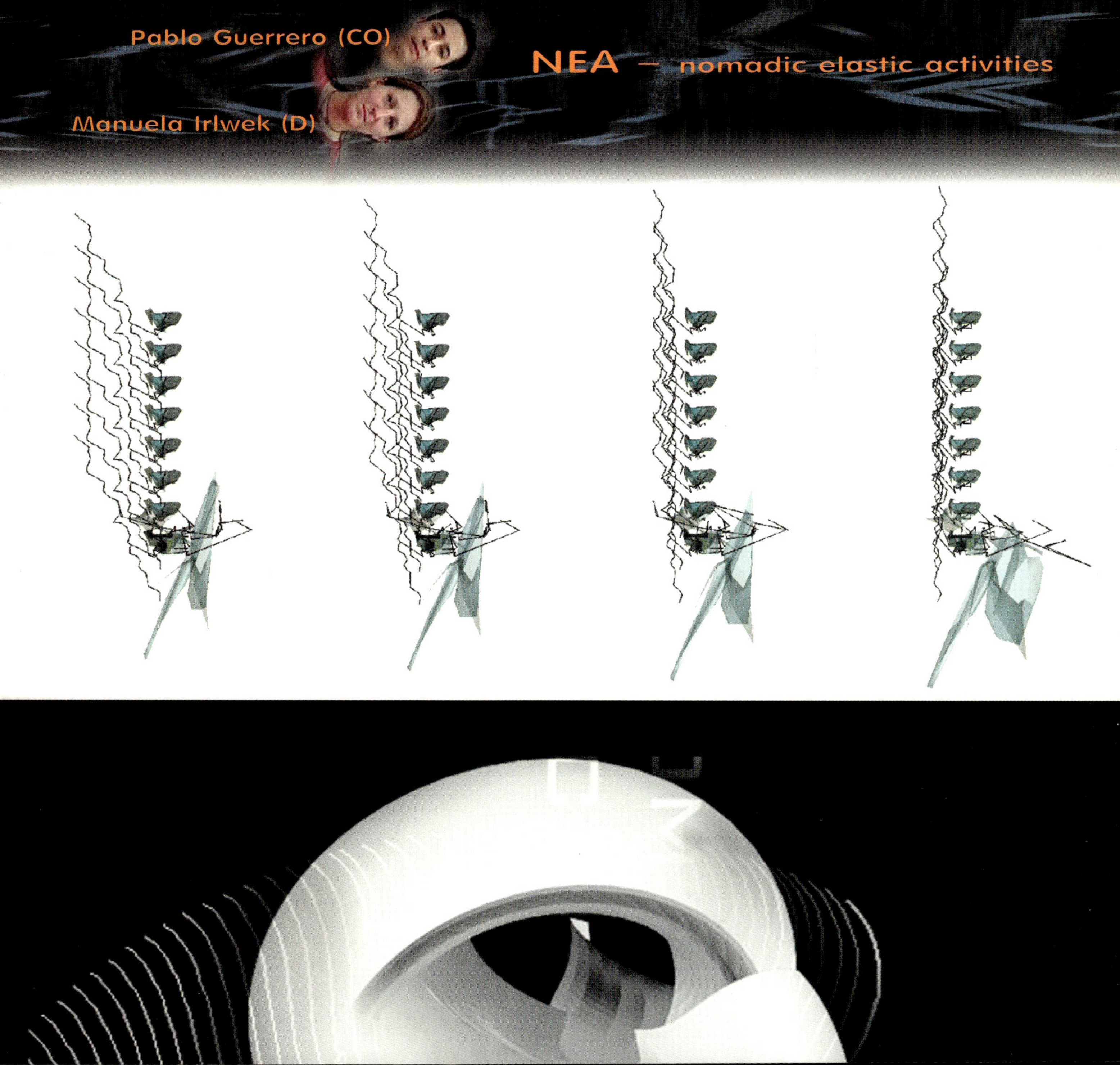
Pablo Guerrero (CO)
Manuela Irlwek (D)
NEA – nomadic elastic activities

NOMADIC...E(LAS
(LASTIC)VENT...
ACTIVITIES

WB
weatherama.com
Edmonds

NOMADIC...E(LASTIC)VENT.
NOMADIC...E(LASTIC)VENT...ACTIVITIES
TIC)VENT...ACTIVITIES
nea
WHEN LIFE PRODUCE REAL IMAGES >
THE FORM OF THE STADIUM AS A VIRTUAL MOVEMENT
MERGES REAL AND PROJECTED ACTIVITIES - IMAGES>
TRANSFORMS TO MATERIAL > FLOORS CEILINGS
MERGE TOGETHER BECOME FURNITURE > VIRTUAL
REALITY TRANSFORMS AND FORMS ACTING IN
PERCEPTION EXPANT TO AN EVENT OF SENSES >
SENSES ARE VISIBLE >
HYBRIDISATION OF HUMANITY AND ARCHITECTURE >
ARCHITECTURE REMAINS FLUID
DIFFERENT ACTIVITIES AT MULITIPLE PLACES ARE
REINFORMED VIA LOCALISED DATA > THIS IS LOOPING
BACK TO THE EFFECTOR - THE STADIUM>
THE PROCESS REFRESHES ITSELF AND GENERATES IN
RELATION TO TIME MULTIPLE IMAGES>
THE STADIUM IS MERGED INTO A NETWORK OF IMAGES>
SUB-LOCAL EVENTS TRANSFORM TO INDIVUDUAL
MOMENTS OF TURBULENCE> SCALING MEANS TO
TRANSFORM IMPULSED DATA IN RELATION TO
MASS-EVENTS OR HOME TV>
AUDIENCE - MASS - PROJECTED IMAGES ARE MERGED
TOGETHER TO A LIFE EVENT> THE CONCEPT PROCESSED
FROM A LOCALISED EVENT TO DYNAMIC TERRITORIES.

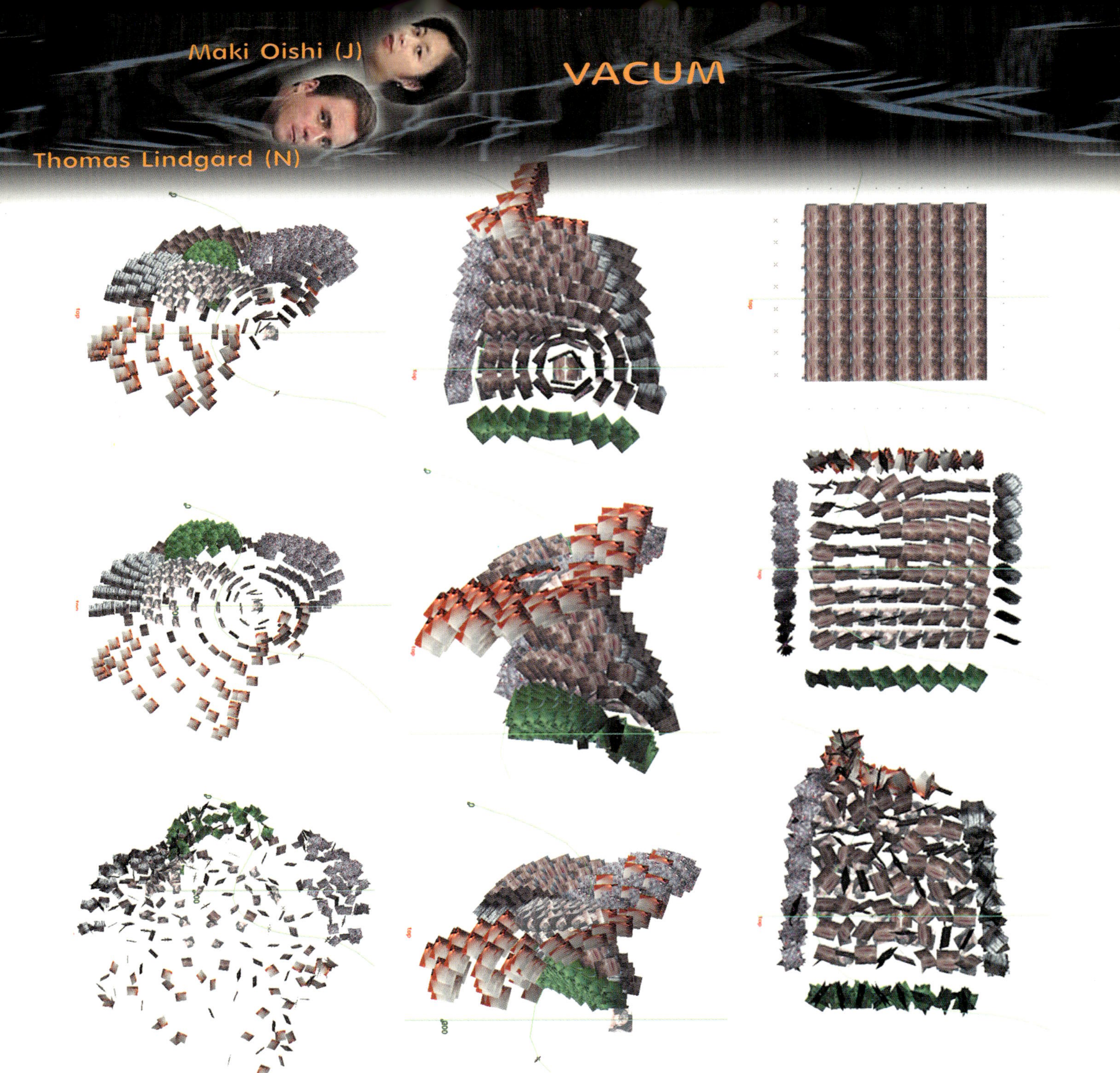
Maki Oishi (J)
Thomas Lindgård (N)
VACUM

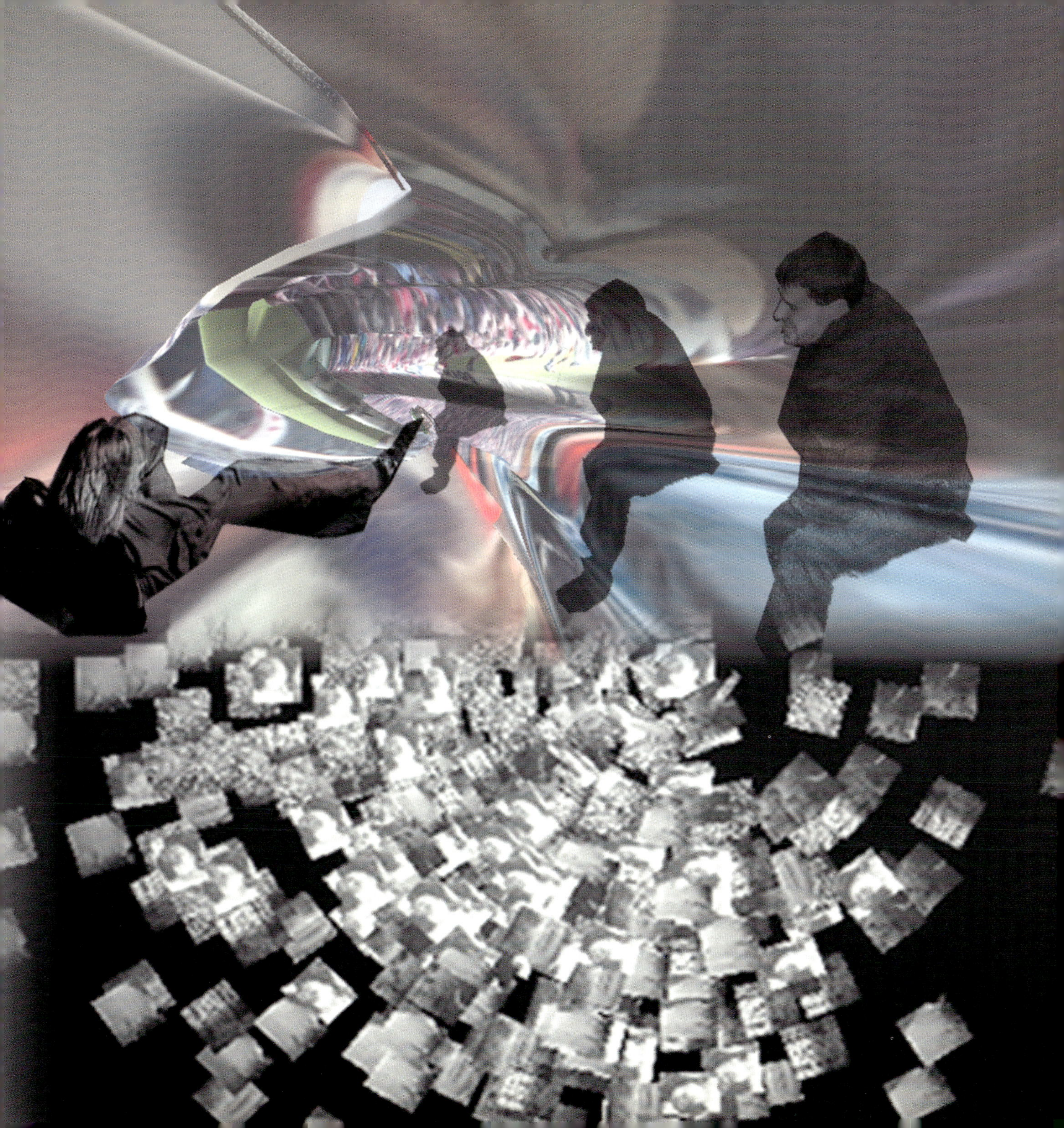

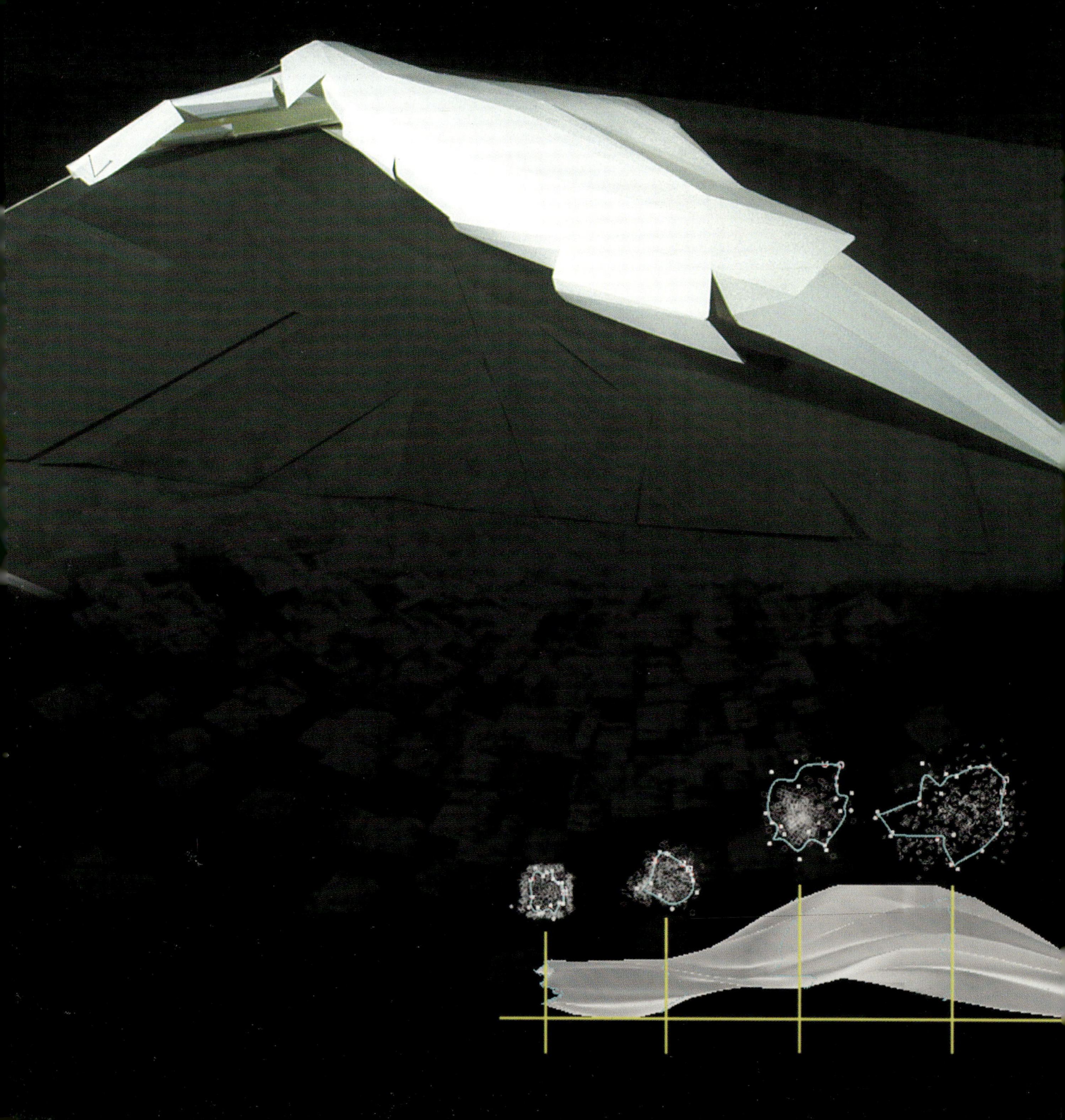

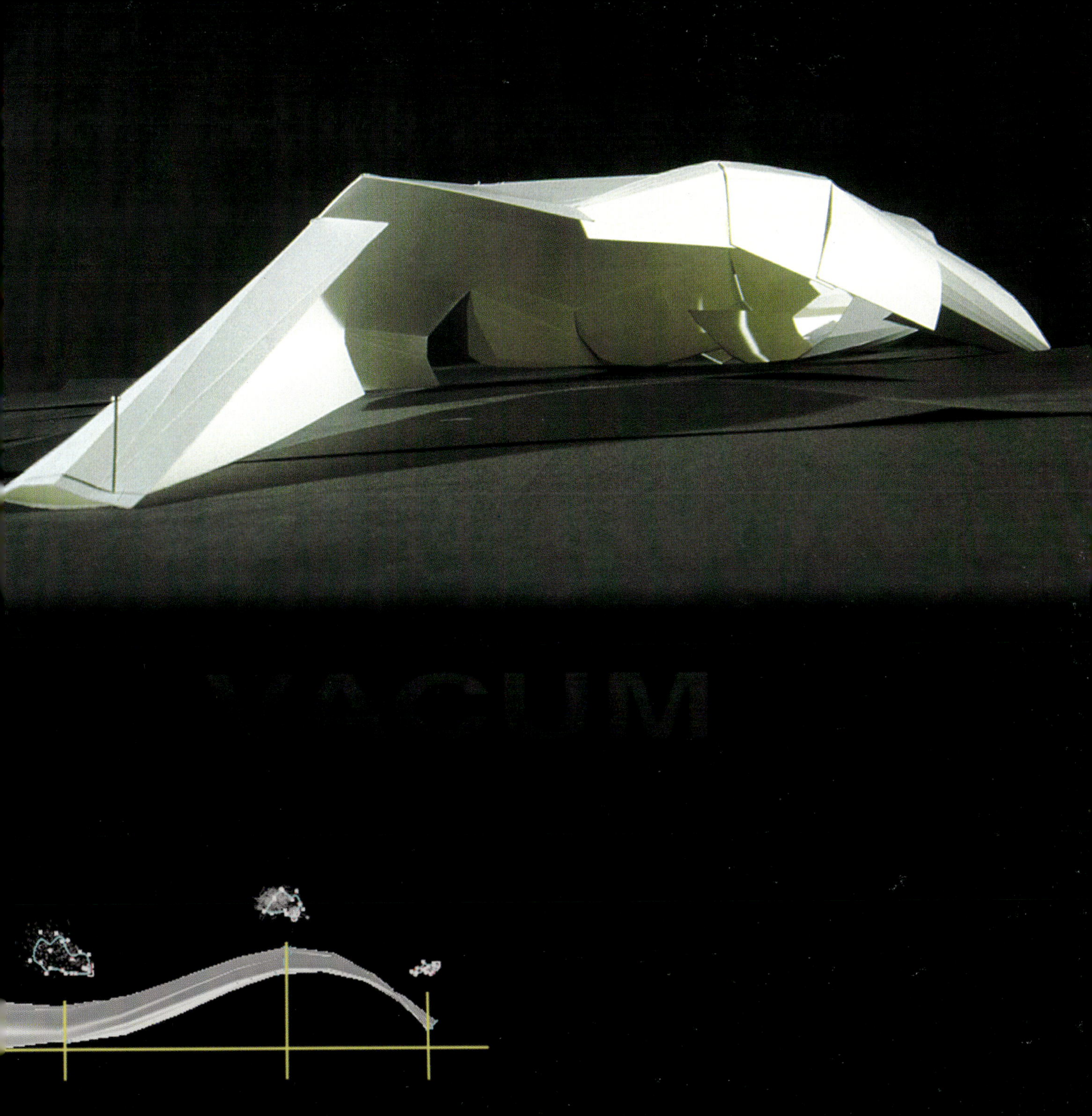
VACUM

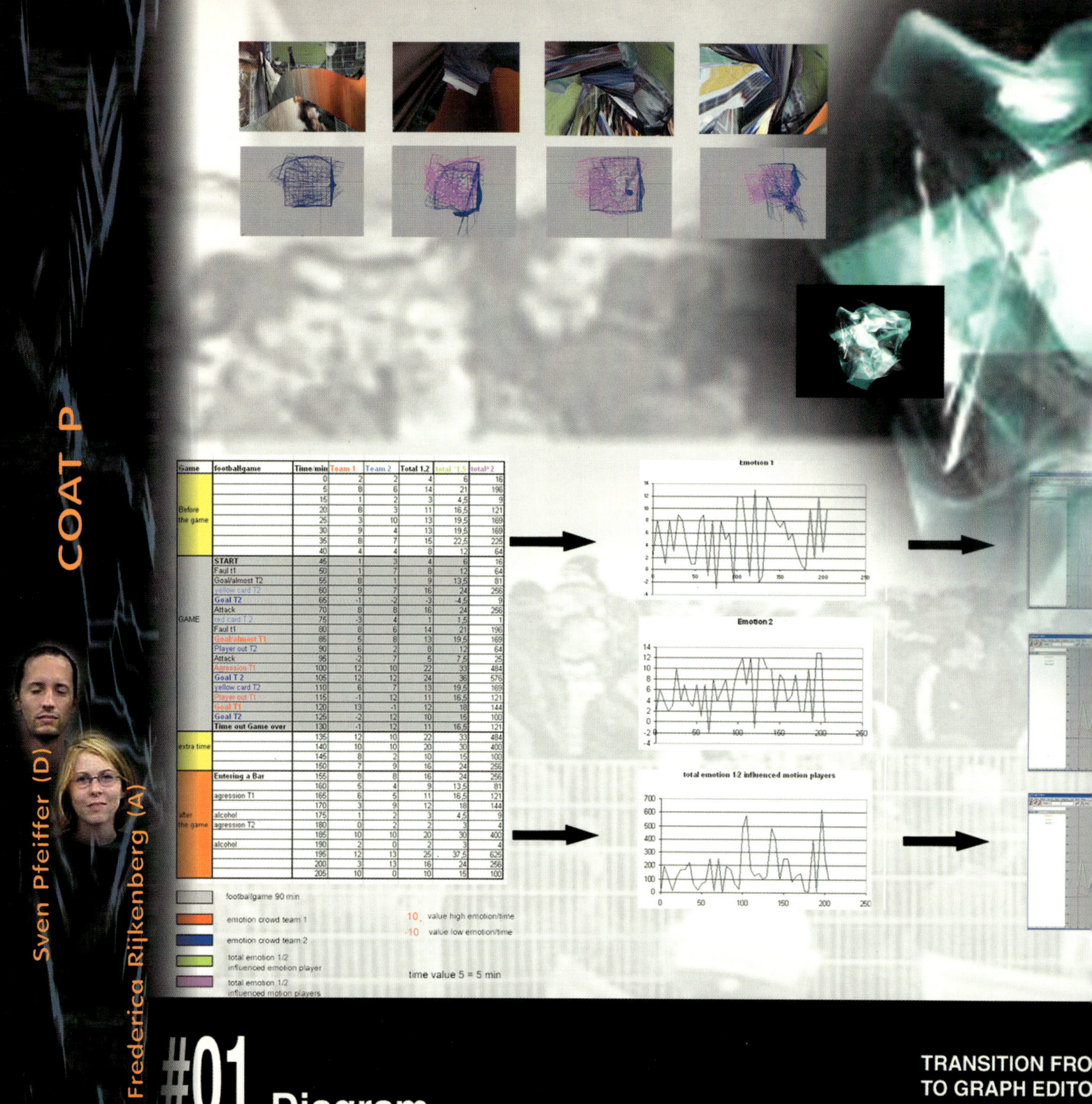

Game	footballgame	Time/min	Team 1	Team 2	Total 1,2	total *1,5	total^2
Before the game		0	2	2	4	6	16
		5	8	6	14	21	196
		15	1	2	3	4,5	9
		20	8	3	11	16,5	121
		25	3	10	13	19,5	169
		30	9	4	13	19,5	169
		35	8	7	15	22,5	225
		40	4	4	8	12	64
GAME	START	45	1	3	4	6	16
	Faul t1	50	1	7	8	12	64
	Goal/almost T2	55	8	1	9	13,5	81
	yellow card T2	60	9	7	16	24	256
	Goal T2	65	-1	-2	-3	-4,5	9
	Attack	70	8	8	16	24	256
	red card T 2	75	-3	4	1	1,5	1
	Faul t1	80	8	6	14	21	196
	Goal/almost T1	85	5	8	13	19,5	169
	Player out T2	90	6	2	8	12	64
	Attack	95	-2	7	5	7,5	25
	Agression T1	100	12	10	22	33	484
	Goal T 2	105	12	12	24	36	576
	yellow card T2	110	6	7	13	19,5	169
	Player out T1	115	-1	12	11	16,5	121
	Goal T1	120	13	-1	12	18	144
	Goal T2	125	-2	12	10	15	100
	Time out Game over	130	-1	12	11	16,5	121
extra time		135	12	10	22	33	484
		140	10	10	20	30	400
		145	8	2	10	15	100
		150	7	9	16	24	256
after the game	Entering a Bar	155	8	8	16	24	256
		160	5	4	9	13,5	81
	agression T1	165	6	5	11	16,5	121
		170	3	9	12	18	144
	alcohol	175	1	2	3	4,5	9
	agression T2	180	0	2	2	3	4
		185	10	10	20	30	400
	alcohol	190	2	0	2	3	4
		195	12	13	25	37,5	625
		200	3	13	16	24	256
		205	10	0	10	15	100

footballgame 90 min
emotion crowd team 1
emotion crowd team 2
total emotion 1/2 influenced emotion player
total emotion 1/2 influenced motion players

10 value high emotion/time
-10 value low emotion/time

time value 5 = 5 min

#01 Diagram

TRANSITION FRO
TO GRAPH EDITO

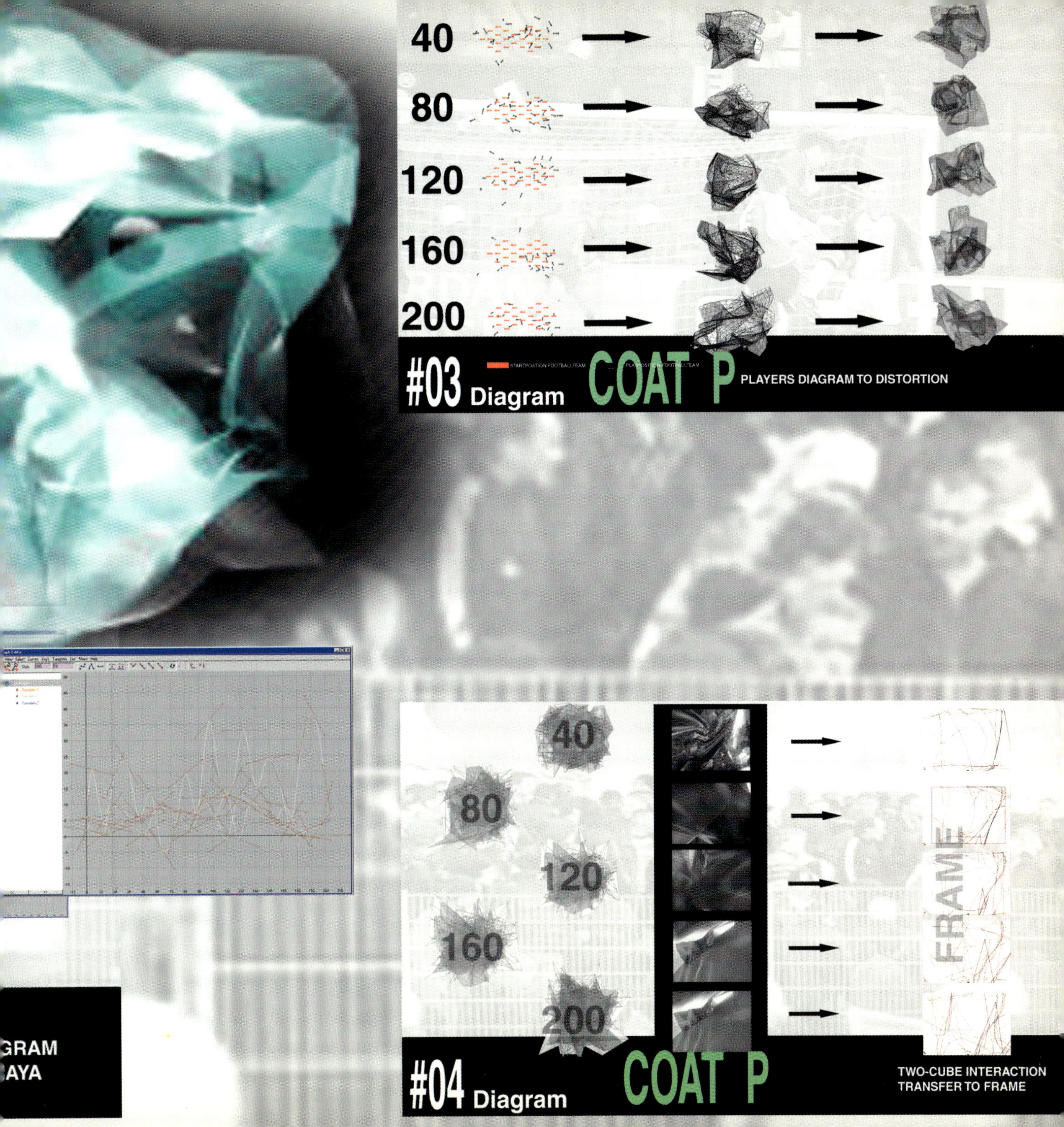
40
80
120
160
200
#03 Diagram
COAT P
PLAYERS DIAGRAM TO DISTORTION
40
80
120
160
200
FRAME
#04 Diagram
COAT P
TWO-CUBE INTERACTION
TRANSFER TO FRAME
GRAM
AYA

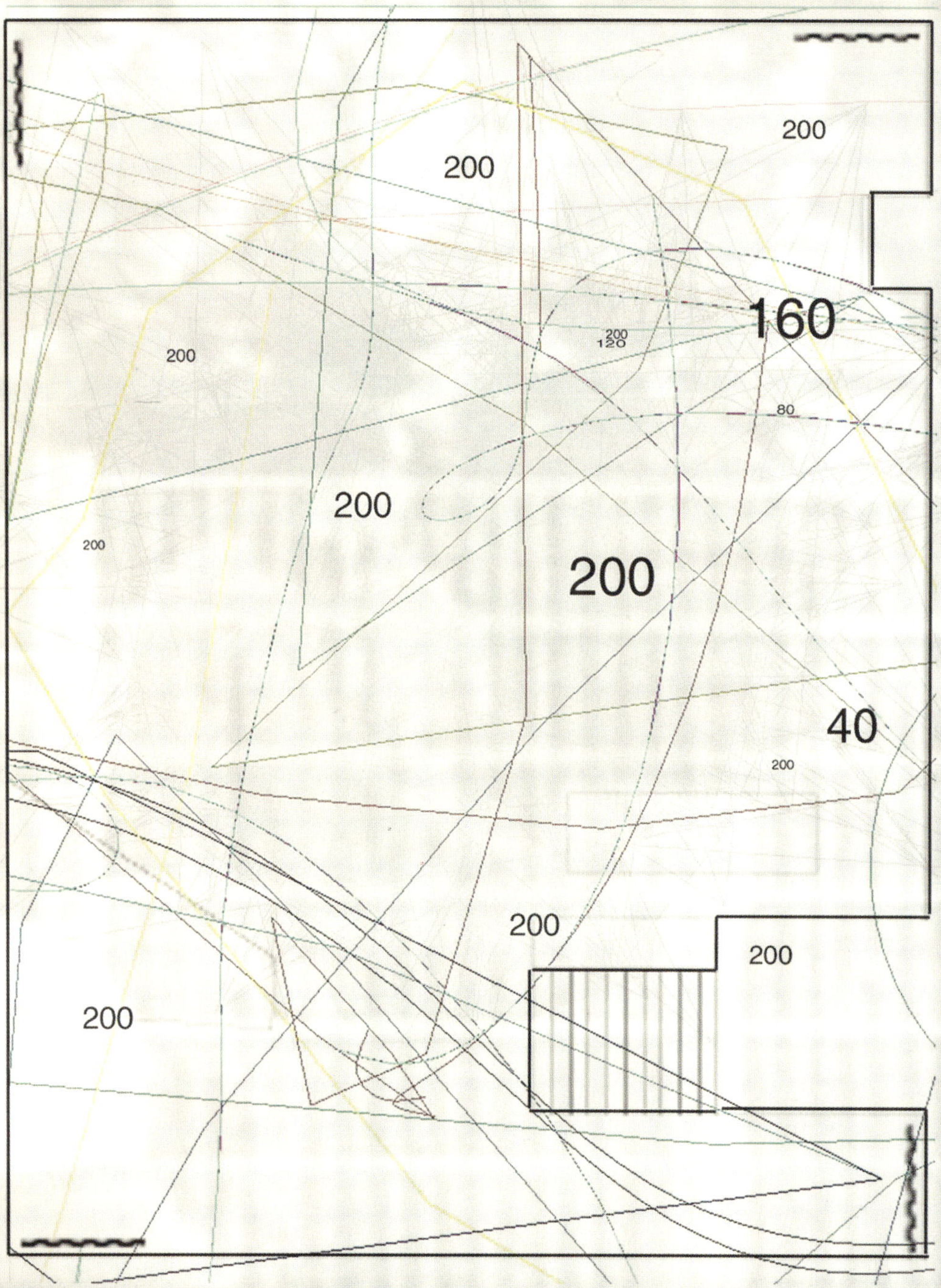
200
200
160
200
120
200
80
200
200
200
40
200
200
200
200

160

200

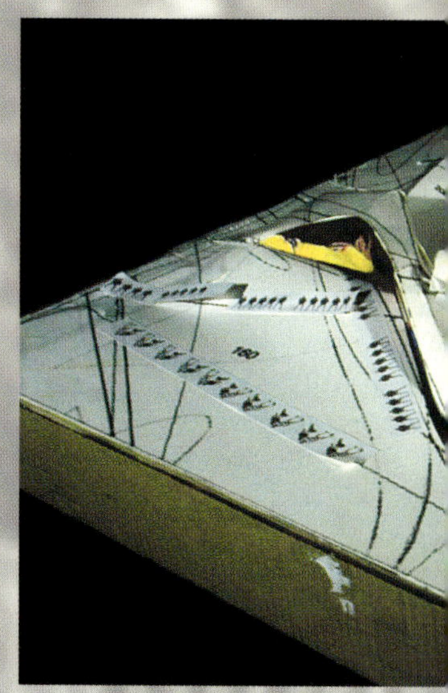

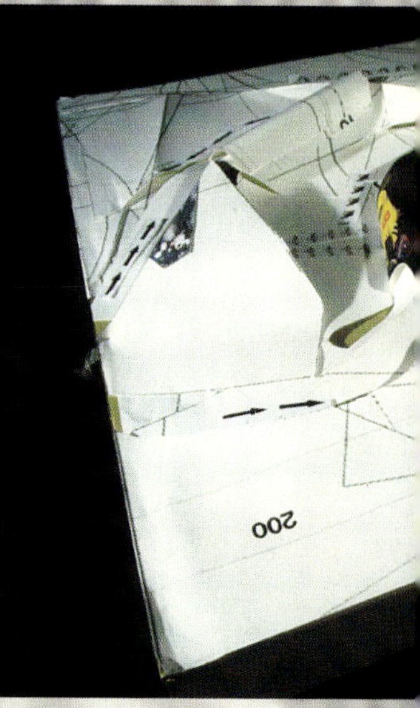

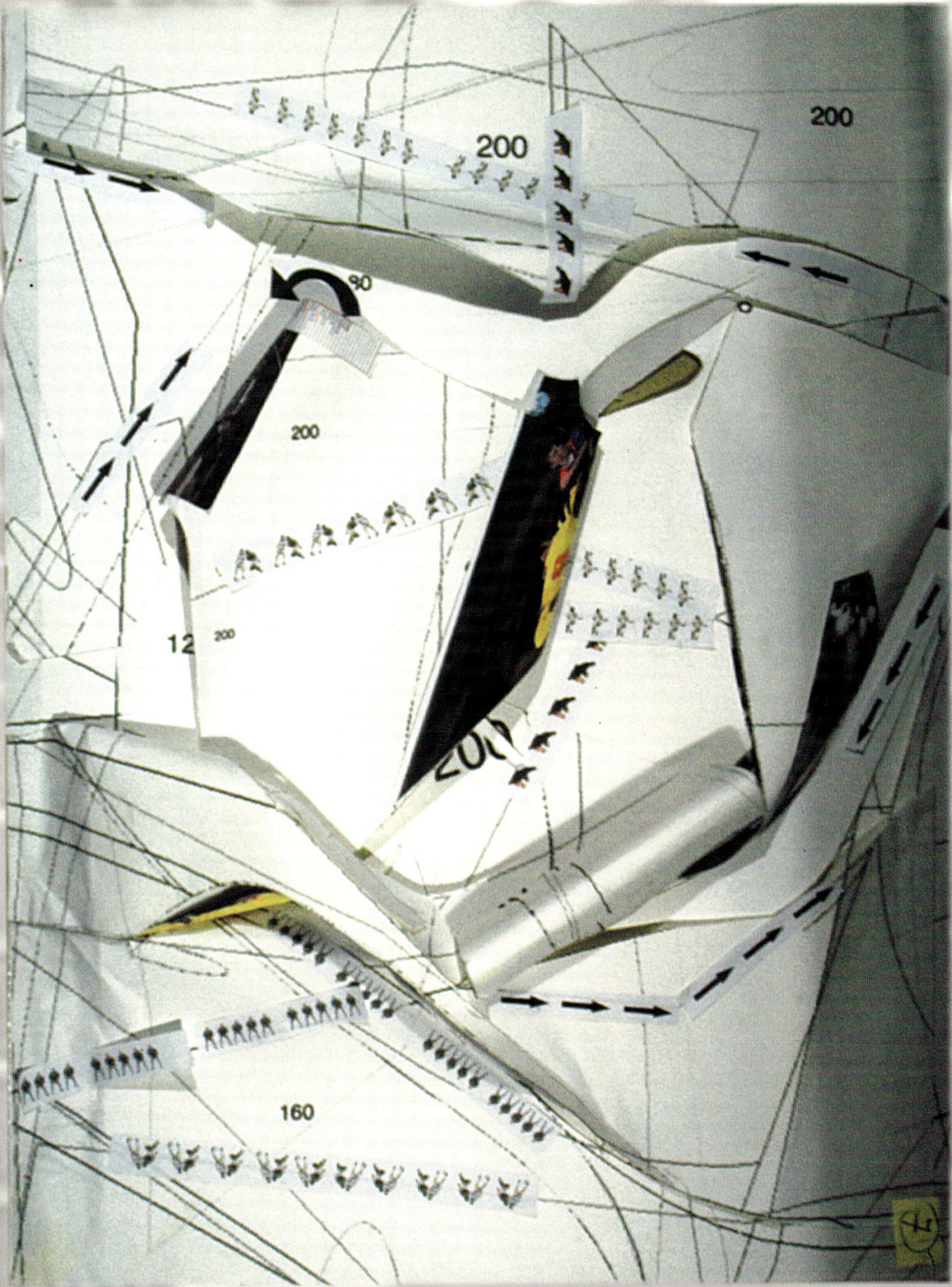

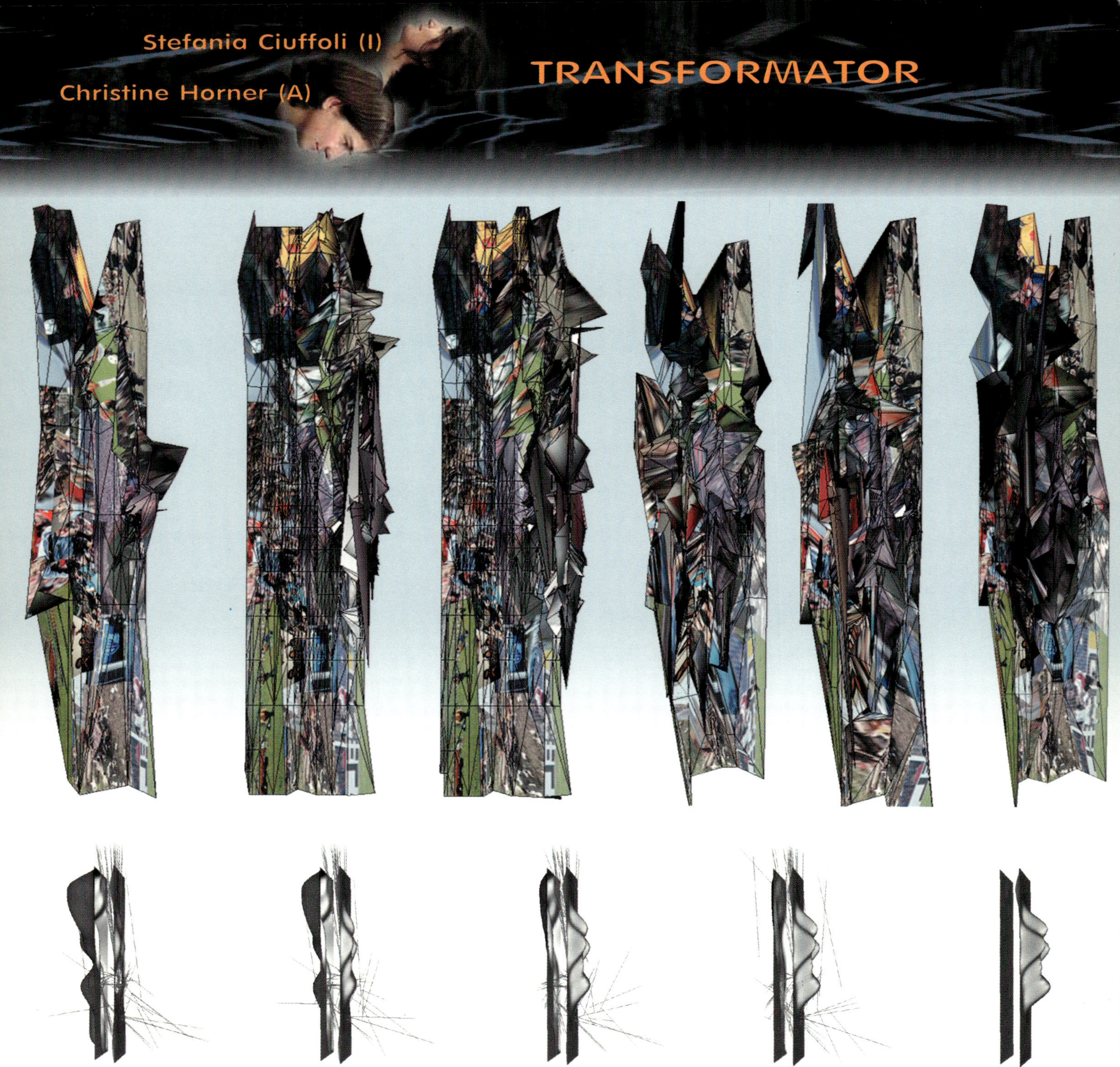
Stefania Ciuffoli (I)
Christine Horner (A)
TRANSFORMATOR

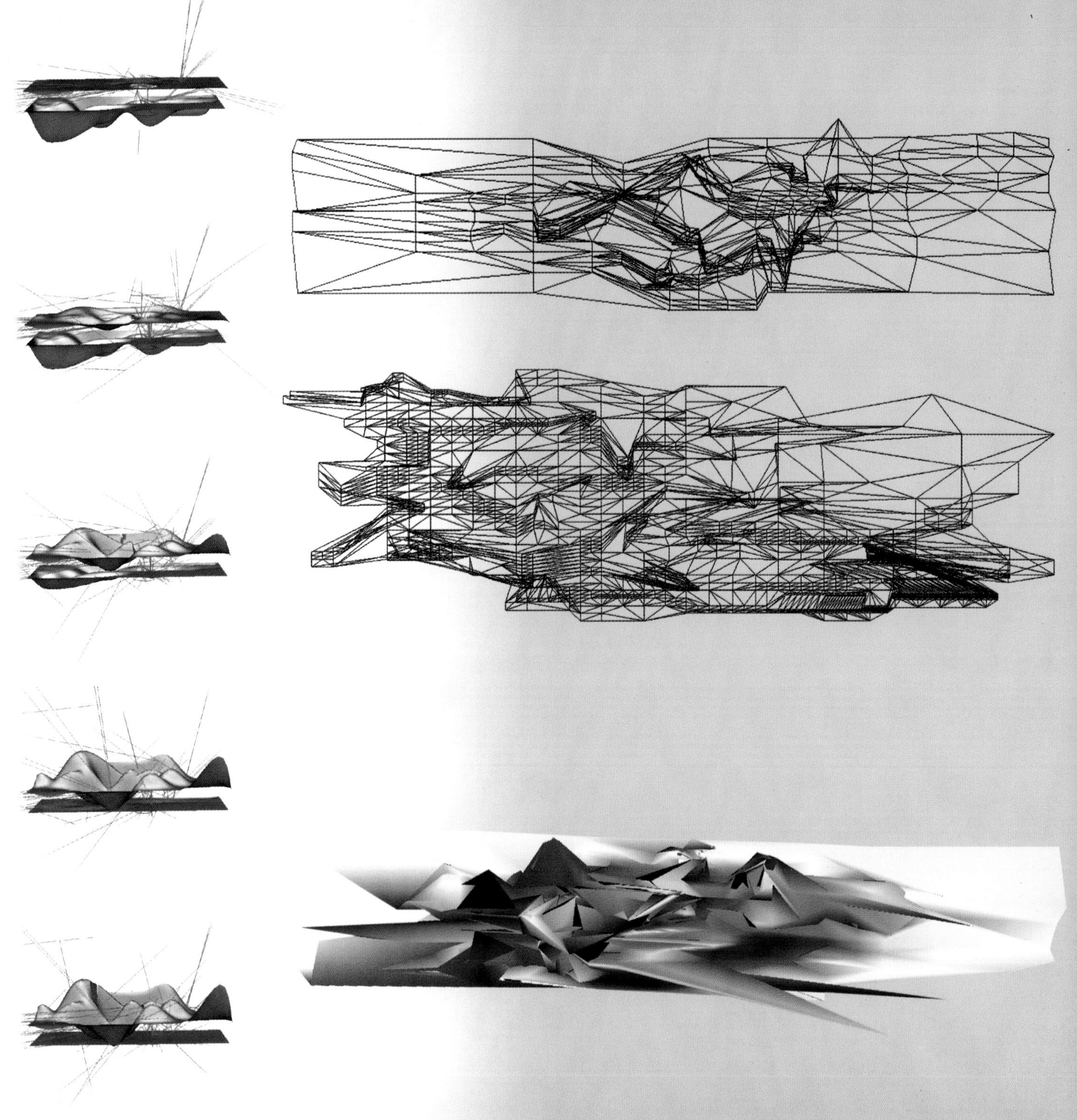

SYSTEM 1_CONNE

ENERGY

SYSTEM 2_CON

TION WITH THE STADIUM
EMOTION, SPEED, PULSE, SOUND
.ENERGY. .ENERGY
ECTION WITH THE TOWN
REACTIONS, RADIO, SCREENS, TV

Editors
Joke Brouwer, Lars Spuybroek and Joan Almekinders
Text corrections by Laura Marz

Design
Joke Brouwer

© Photography: Joan Almekinders and Anke van Helden
© Text: Lars Spuybroek and Bob Lang

Masters
Lars Spuybroek, NOX, Rotterdam
Bob Lang, ARUP, London

Maya Tutors
Joan Almekinders, NOX (Maya tutorial)
Gemma Koppen, NOX
Ernst Janssen Groesbeek, TU Delft,
Thomas Dubbink, TU Delft
Simon van Vegten, TU Delft
Martin Ketellapper, TU Delft
Remco Wilcke, TU Delft (Maya tutorial)
Meik van Noordt, V2_Lab

System Operators
Ramon-Felon Venne, TU Delft·
Roderick Guèpin, NAI
Godard van Randwijck, NAI

Project Organization NAI
Caatje Peeters, Project Coordinator
Rinske Brand, Project Assistant
Arlette Feltz Süssenbach, Project Assistant
Paul van den Berg, Technical Assistant
Joost de Munk, Technical Assistant
John Wuisman, Caterer

Sponsors
The master class is organized in collaboration with the Netherlands Architecture Institute, Technical University Delft (Faculty Architecture, Chair Technical Design & Informatics), V2_Lab and is made possible by Alias/Wavefront, Interactive Visual Systems and Harolds Grafik.

With special thanks to
Bart Lootsma, Joost Meuwissen and Matthijs Bouw (One Architecture), Meindert Booy (Van den Broek en Bakema), Anne Nigten (V2_Lab), Michelle Provoost (NAI), Euro2000, Stadion Feijenoord, WaterLand Neeltje Jans, NJHC City Hostel, Trossen Los Grafisch Ontwerp and Technical Department NAI.

www.nai.nl

© NAI Publishers, Rotterdam 2001
All rights reserved. No part of this publication may be reproduced, stored in a retrieval system, or transmitted in any form or by any means, electronic, mechanical, photocopying, recording or otherwise, without the prior written permission of the publisher.

Available in North, South and Central America through D.A.P./Distributed Art Publishers Inc, 155 Sixth Avenue 2nd Floor, New York, NY 10013-1507, Tel. 212 627.1999 Fax 212 627.9484.

ISBN 90-5662-168-8